JEWISH THINKERS

General Editor: Arthur Hertzberg

Bialik

Bialik

David Aberbach

Grove Press
New York

Published by Grove Press
a division of Wheatland Corporation
920 Broadway
New York, N.Y. 10010

Library of Congress Cataloging-in-Publication Data

Aberbach, David, 1954—
    Bialik / David Aberbach.—1st ed.
        p. cm.—(Jewish thinkers)
    Bibliography: p.
    Includes index.
    ISBN 0-8021-1062-2
    1. Bialik, Hayyim Nahman, 1873–1934—Criticism and
interpretation.
    I. Title. II. Series.
PJ5053.B52A63 1988
892.4'15—dc19   88-4562
                                                           CIP

Manufactured in the United States of America
First Edition 1988
10 9 8 7 6 5 4 3 2 1

To Mimi

with much love

ACKNOWLEDGEMENTS

Although this book was written especially for the Jewish Thinkers series, it began life in 1975 as an Oxford thesis and later developed in the form of articles for *Encounter*, *Prooftexts*, *International Review of Psycho-Analysis*, *Hebrew Union College Annual* and *Moznayim*. I remain indebted to my Oxford teachers during the formative period: the late Dr Meir Gertner, Mr Francis Warner and Dr David Patterson.

I am also most grateful to many others who read the book, or parts of it, at various stages in its growth and who made many helpful suggestions: Dr Glenda Abramson, Mrs Sonia Argyle, Sir Isaiah Berlin, Professors John Bayley, John Carey, David Daiches and the late Richard Ellmann, Judy Gough, Dr Michael Hilton, Rabbi Dr Arthur Hertzberg, Dr Albert Hourani, Miss Deborah Maccoby, Professor Harold Merskey, Betty Palmer, Professor Ezra Spicehandler, Dr Anthony Storr and Dr Leon Yudkin.

Thanks are also due to Dr Martin Gilbert for preparing the map on p. x for this book.

I also wish to record my gratitude to the librarians of the libraries that I used: Bet Bialik, Tel Aviv; Bodleian Library, Oxford; King's College, Cambridge; Kressel Archives, Yarnton Manor, Yarnton, Oxford; Houghton Library, Harvard University; National Library, Jerusalem; Tavistock Clinic Library, London.

Acknowledgement is due to Faber and Faber for permission to quote from 'Ash Wednesday' and 'The Waste Land' from *Collected Poems 1909–1962* by T. S. Eliot.

Finally, and most important, I thank Peter and Martine Halban for their encouragement and help during the writing of this book.

Note on Transliteration

The general system of transliteration has been used. The dot under the H has been included to denote the Hebrew letter *chet* and has been used where essential to pronunciation or meaning. A superior comma has been used to denote the Hebrew letters *aleph* and *eyin*, e.g. Ba'al.

CONTENTS

Acknowledgements   vii

Introduction   xi

1   The Man and the Legend   1

2   The Background   19

3   Literary Roots   37

4   Romantic–National Poet   56

5   National Figure   97

6   Poet of Private Grief   108

7   Conclusion   114

Notes   120

Bibliography   132

Index   138

SWEDEN

FINLAND

Lake
Onega

Lake
Ladoga

St.Petersburg

Baltic Sea

BALTIC PROVINCES

Nizhni
Novgorod
(Gorky) →

Moscow

LITHUANIA

Kovno
Vilna
Volozhin
Minsk

T S A R I S T

GERMANY

Bialystok
Pripet
marshes

R U S S I A

Warsaw
Siedlce
POLISH
PROVINCES
Brest-
Litovsk
Gomel

Sosnowiec
VOLHYNIA
Korosten
Malin
Radomyshl
(Radi)
Kiev

Cracow
Zhitomir
Pereyaslav
Kharkov

Kattowitz
Gorovshtzin

AUSTRIA-
HUNGARY
Zashkov
Yekaterinoslav

UKRAINE

Balta
Yelizavetgrad
Rostov

RUMANIA
Kishinev

BESSARABIA
Melitopol

Odessa
Sea of
Azov

CRIMEA

Feodosiya

Black Sea

─·─·─ Russia's western border, 1815-1914

········· Northern and eastern limit of the
Pale of Jewish Settlement

0   miles   200
0   kilometres   300

© Martin Gilbert 1988

INTRODUCTION

Half a century after his death, Chaim Nachman Bialik is still frequently described as the finest and most influential modern Hebrew poet. He first became famous for poems written in Tsarist Russia during the pogroms of 1903–6, and for the rest of his life he was hailed, almost uncritically and much against his will, as the poet laureate of Jewish nationalism. He was also regarded as one of the chief Jewish cultural influences of his age. Today he is largely forgotten, except in Israel where schoolchildren learn that Bialik is the national poet of the Jewish people, and where there is hardly a town without a street named for him.

The reader who knows no Hebrew may find Bialik's achievement and influence hard to fathom. English versions of his works are mostly antiquated and, in any case, the richness and subtlety of his style, which depends greatly on allusions to classical Hebrew literature, lose much in translation. (Bialik once compared translation to kissing through a handkerchief.) The translator cannot do justice to the immense love and care with which Bialik wrote Hebrew. Nor can he hope to show precisely how well Bialik in his best poems suits form to content, or capture accurately Bialik's sure instinct for the rhythm and music of Hebrew, or the vast range of his rhymes, metres and moods. The age in which Bialik lived, and which is constantly reflected in his works—the Russian Pale of Settlement, the pogroms, the decline and fall of the Romanovs, the rise of Zionism and of Hebrew as a living language—is, moreover, not well known to most English readers.

Added to these difficulties are the bewildering variety and complexity of Bialik's career, or careers, for he was not only a poet, but also, at various times, a writer of fiction, scholar, essayist, businessman, editor, director of a publishing company, educator, children's writer, translator and, by the end of his life, a public man for all purposes. Each of these might have added up to a career in itself. These roles are interconnected, though it might be said of Bialik, as W. B. Yeats wrote of Major Robert Gregory, that he did each, 'as though he had but that one trade alone'. In combining the roles of poet and public man, Bialik closely resembles Yeats, Richard Ellmann's assessment of whom is applicable to Bialik: 'He spent much of his life attempting to understand the deep contradictions within his mind, and was perhaps most alive to that which separated the man of action lost in reverie from the man of reverie who could not quite find himself in action'.[1]

The fragmented nature of Bialik's career mirrors his life story and his inner life. He once wrote that his life consisted of 'nothing but broken tunes of various instruments, each one playing for itself, and happening to be at the same place—and if they formed one partly whole tune, it's a miracle.'[2] Like Yeats, too, Bialik made no secret of the often inseparable links between his art and his life. For this reason, a knowledge of the poet's life is virtually indispensable to understanding his art. Unfortunately there is as yet no full-length biography or critical study of Bialik in English. Fischel Lachower's standard Hebrew biography, while still extremely useful, is unfinished and out of date.

The chief aims of this book are to set out the main facts about Bialik's life and career, and to explore the historical, social and literary background to his spectacular rise as a Romantic-nationalist poet. Yet Bialik's enduring greatness is not as a national poet. The fascination of his art lies precisely in his ambivalence to his national role, his obsession with intensely private themes, and the unexpected interplay between the legendary public figure and the confessional lyric poet.

THE MAN AND THE LEGEND

The misery at home, the bitter orphanhood, weighed heavily on me. I was invited by relatives to a wedding party. The light and music filled my heart, which thirsted so badly to feel joy again. Like a madman I danced barefoot to the music. I forgot myself, but my heart longed to join a circle, to cleave to something, to belong. Though my hands were stretched out, no one took them. Pushed and struggling from ring to ring, I didn't see that I was slowly being pushed out of the door. I danced alone in the courtyard by the entrance. For a long time I went round until mother found me and took me home.[1]

Practically all that we know about Bialik's childhood and adolescence comes from Bialik himself and was written down many years after the events described. Though the details are not always reliable—at times they are openly mythical—the deep feeling expressed in the poetry may itself be taken as a trustworthy gauge of his inner biography. Bialik was born on 11 January 1873 in the Ukrainian village of Radi (Radomyshl) to Joseph Isaac Bialik, a timber merchant, and his wife, Dinah Priva.[2] Both parents had been married previously. Bialik was the second of three surviving children; at least two other siblings died during his early childhood. Like Wordsworth, he remembered his first years as a lost paradise whose splendour he could still occasionally glimpse and recapture in his poetry: the paradise did not last. When Bialik was five, his father's business failed and the family moved to the nearby town of Zhitomir, capital of Volhynia. Joseph Isaac had family there, including his father, Jacob Moses, a venerable, wealthy businessman who had retired many years previously to devote his life to prayer and study.[3]

Here Bialik's father set up as a tavern keeper. In the poem 'Avi' (My Father, 1928), Bialik remembered him studying the Mishna while drunkards staggered in and out of the tavern.[4] Quiet and spiritual, he was the antithesis of the mother, a deeply emotional woman who was chiefly remembered in Radi and Zhitomir for her wailing at funerals. Bialik claimed to have inherited the qualities of both parents.[5] He seems also to have connected the dual nature of his poetry—the tender reflective lyrics and the contrasting poems of thunderous emotion—with the vexing opposites of his early life.

Zhitomir in the 1870s was in a state of economic depression. Business went poorly and the father fell ill and died—Bialik was seven at the time and this loss had a momentous impact on his character and creativity. 'If only my father had lived,' he wrote many years later to a friend:

> If only I had grown on his knees ... he would have educated me in his way, according to my abilities. He would have taught me: this is the way for you to go, and I would not have been torn into ten pieces, my steps would have been sure on this chosen path. I would have had a settled mind, a man among men, knowing his worth and his place, happy and successful all his days. But because my father died and I was raised by my grandfather, my education passed into the hands of strangers and my defeat was total.[6]

Perhaps equally traumatic was his separation from his mother, who was unable to support her children single-handed. Soon after her husband's death she turned Bialik and his sister over to her in-laws in Zhitomir and went to live with relatives in the far-off village of Zashkov. Bright and mischievous, in mourning for his parents (though he did see his mother occasionally), Bialik found life with his aged grandparents almost unbearably stifling. In a posthumous fragment, he described his grandfather:

> This old man, of blessed memory, mortified himself in the fear of God, he studied the Torah for its own sake—and educated me in his own way. While he was strict by

nature, like all old men who don't approve of the ebullience of youth, I was naturally bold, like children in general and orphans in particular.[7]

In another posthumous piece, Bialik described the tormenting regime which the old puritan apparently tried to impose on him, the endless learning equated with virtue, the Talmud, Zohar, prayers each day,

> A hundred blessings, bundle upon bundle of *mitzvot* [commandments] and the minutiae of *mitzvot*, and the minutiae of the minutiae, from the day the Lord created the Chumash [Five Books of Moses] until the last book of laws or ethics was written down ... And all this labour the Jew is obliged to undertake, is not free to be rid of and escape, even for one hour.[8]

By the time he reached the age of thirteen, Bialik was regarded as an intellectual prodigy. He studied on his own in the local synagogue and, he recalled, was consulted on questions of Jewish law.

At seventeen he left home, to spend the next sixteen months at the yeshivah (school for advanced study of the Talmud) in the Lithuanian town of Volozhin, one of the greatest centres of Jewish learning in eastern Europe. While at the yeshivah, he began to write Hebrew poetry and prose and learned to read Russian. He came under the sway of Ahad Ha'am ('One of the people', pen name of Asher Ginzburg, 1856–1927), the most influential Hebrew essayist of the age. Intoxicated by his essays, Bialik joined a clandestine Zionist society founded by Ahad Ha'am. 'Every word that Ahad Ha'am wrote,' he recalled several years later, 'seemed to be addressed to me, to my innermost thoughts. I could feel that a new era was coming in the world of our literature.'[9] He published his first Hebrew article in 1891 in the prestigious journal *Ha-Melitz* (The Advocate), on the concept of a spiritual centre for the Jewish people in the Land of Israel.[10]

Although Bialik was a talented student, the yeshivah was too narrow for his taste. The intensity of his studies diminished as he became increasingly impatient: 'In the first days of spring I would escape the yeshivah and race like a madman through the streets and alleys of Volozhin, my heart struggling like a trapped bird: I must get away.'[11] His ambition at this time was to gain a university degree or qualify as a rabbi in a modern orthodox rabbinical seminary in Berlin. (He had been turned down by the latter as he had no high school diploma.) To prepare himself for these goals he decided to go to Odessa, at that time the centre of Hebrew literary life and of the nascent Zionist movement. In September 1891 he left Volozhin without telling his grandfather, who would have totally condemned his ambitions, having written letters to be forwarded periodically to his grandparents by his friends at the yeshivah. Once he arrived in Odessa, however, he found that his plans could not easily be put into practice:

> Wild, shy, dumb, unmannered, I came to Odessa—penniless, with only vague hopes—for no sooner had I arrived than I predicted that I would get nowhere. In a big city like this, a boy like me would get lost. And that's how it was: for six months I wandered like a lost lamb in Odessa. Starved and tormented, I lived in cellars with victims of tuberculosis. No one knew.[12]

Yet in Odessa the course of his life was changed by a series of fateful encounters. He met his idol Ahad Ha'am, as well as M. L. Lilienblum (1843–1910), one of the leaders of the proto-Zionist Ḥibbat Zion (Lovers of Zion) movement, and his future friend and collaborator J. H. Ravnitzky (1863–1943). His poems made a great impression on the Hebrew circle in Odessa—at this time good Hebrew poetry was scarce. Several months later, Ravnitzky published one of these poems, 'El ha-Tzippor' (To the Bird), a sentimental lyric of longing for Zion, in an anthology of Hebrew writings. By the age of nineteen, Bialik was recognized as the most promising of the younger Hebrew poets.

Meanwhile, Bialik had returned to Zhitomir to find his grandfather and his elder half-brother dying. A period of grief and confusion was followed by happier times. In the following year, in June 1893, he married Manya Averbach, the daughter of a well-to-do timber merchant—it was an arranged marriage. In her memoirs, Manya recalled that her father had wanted to further Bialik's ambitions in Berlin but, failing that, bought him some forest land in the woods of Korosten, near Kiev. For the next four years Bialik worked for his father-in-law as a timber merchant. Like his father many years previously, he would spend weekdays in the forest and come home for the Sabbath. His isolation spurred his creativity. He wrote profusely, including the long, ambitious poem *Ha-Matmid* (The Talmud Student, 1896–7), based largely on his memories of the Volozhin yeshivah. Many of his overtly 'national' poems, denouncing the Jewish people for their apathy or calling for their revival, were written at this time. His marriage, happy in other respects, was childless, which remained to the end of his life a source of pain, frustration and inferiority.

The First Zionist Congress convened by Theodor Herzl in Basle in 1897 was a watershed in Bialik's growth as a poet. Zionism had already made a considerable impact on the Jews in the Russian empire. The first modern wave of Jewish immigrants to Palestine had come mostly from among the Russian Jews during and after the pogroms of 1881–2. With the creation of the World Zionist Congress by Herzl, the Russian delegates, representing nearly 400 Zionist societies, constituted nearly one-third of the total delegates. Now that Zionism had become an international political movement, the revival of Hebrew grew in importance as the national language of the Jewish people. Bialik was looked upon increasingly as the the poet-prophet of Jewish nationalism, a modern Isaiah. Many of his poems of this period are responses to the extraordinary changes which were taking place in the Jewish world, but only a few offer hope: in many a dark despair is evident. He wrote to Ravnitzky that his strongest urge was to mourn. Looking at this confession alongside the poems, the reader may feel how closely Bialik's sense of national grief was bound up with his own unresolved childhood griefs:

Sometimes I doubt that my writings and those of others like me are any use at all. Whom are they for? What are they for? Our ancient nation is broken, annihilated, and there is no modern Jeremiah to compose the final, terrible lament... Songs of revival are lies, falsehood and lies! We have not mourned adequately and we wait for the great poet to do so. We still don't have a jeremiad for the ruined nation, and it must come. It will engulf the whole dispersion with tears and become an eternal lament.[13]

For all the despair which dominates much of Bialik's poetry, he was seen for most of his lifetime and after as the poet of hope and revival. This paradox reverberates all through his writings. For example, his essay 'Giluy ve-Khisuy be-Lashon' (Revelation and Concealment in Language, 1915) is a fascinating exposition of the role of language in dealing with the *Angst* which allegedly underlies existence. Language, Bialik writes, does not reveal one's inmost feelings but plugs the holes of existence through which dark chaos may be glimpsed. For poets, words are a kind of armour or charm to ward off the devils of chronic anxiety. At the same time the chaos beckons. Far from being a confident poet of national revival, Bialik here expresses a particularly modern dilemma, that of a man who has lost his faith in God and had found nothing else to believe in with total faith:

Eternal darkness alone, so frightening, draws the heart of man incessantly, arousing in him the hidden longing to glimpse it—just for a moment. All afraid, all drawn to it. We build walls of words to hide it. And our fingernails go to work, scratching at the walls to make a tiny hole to see what lies beyond. But it's useless! No sooner is the hole made than a new partition, a new word, blocks the view... As long as man lives and breathes and acts, he fills the emptiness. Everything is fine, superficially. 'I'm all right, thanks.' The ebb and flow of daily life is nothing but a constant effort to divert. Each moment of 'chasing after' is at the same time a 'fleeing from'.[14]

In an interview given not long before his death, Philip Larkin spoke of the affirmative nature of poetry, and his remarks are true of Bialik and of all poets who write in a minor key: 'The substance may be pessimistic or melancholy. But a poem, if it's a good one, is a positive and joyful thing: it represents the mastering, even if just for a moment, of the pessimism and melancholy, and enables you—you the poet, and you, the reader—to go on.'[15]

After the collapse of Bialik's timber business in 1897, he moved to the town of Sosnowiec, near the Prussian border, where he worked as a teacher. His wife remained with her parents in the Kiev area. While continuing to produce poetry of increasingly high quality, Bialik wrote his first Hebrew short story, 'Aryeh Ba'al Guf' (Aryeh the Powerful, 1898) and his first poems in Yiddish, his mother tongue.

In 1900, Bialik moved with his wife to Odessa. His life there was a welter of confusion, false starts, failure, immense triumph, tragedy and, finally, despair. He worked first as a teacher and merchant, later as literary editor of Ha-Shiloah—the foremost Hebrew journal of the time—and as a publisher. In 1901 he helped to found the publishing company Moriah, whose aim was to produce Hebrew educational texts, mainly for schools. That year Bialik's first volume of poems was published in Warsaw.

During the years 1900–11, Bialik reached his full power as a poet. He began with a series of Blakean lyrics, compressed, private and obscure, dominated by his striving after artistic perfection, raising the Hebrew lyric to the level of the great European Romantic poets. National themes are virtually non-existent in these poems. But then, in May 1903, Bialik was commissioned by the Jewish Historical Society of Odessa to visit Kishinev, interview the survivors of the recent pogrom there and write a report describing what had happened. Deeply shocked by what he saw and heard, he retreated to his in-laws' home in Gorovshchin, near Kiev, and instead of the report, wrote the poem Be-Ir ha-Haregah (In the City of Slaughter), a chilling portrait of Kishinev after the massacre. The publication of this poem in Bialik's Hebrew and Yiddish versions and in Ze'ev Jabotinsky's superb Russian translation had a galvanizing impact on Russian Jewry. This poem, more than any other, cemented Bialik's reputation as the national poet of the Jewish people.

Later that year Bialik was appointed co-editor, with the critic and historian Joseph Klausner, of *Ha-Shiloah*, in succession to Ahad Ha'am. For over a year, until January 1905, Bialik was again apart from his wife in Warsaw, where the journal was then being published. He continued this work—with an interruption from 1905 to 1907, when the journal was closed by the government—until 1909.

Be-Ir ha-Haregah was followed by other 'Poems of Wrath', as Bialik later called them, until 1906 when the pogroms ceased. During the same period, he continued to write tender nature poems and passionate lyrics of lost love or love never known. These works culminated in the completion of the poem 'Ha-Brekha' (The Pool) and the composition of the experimental prose-poem *Megillat ha-Esh* (The Scroll of Fire), in the summer of 1905, at the time of the *Potemkin* mutiny and the shelling of Odessa. Bialik never again equalled the creative output of the years 1903–6, and if he had written nothing but these poems, he would still have earned a place in the front ranks of modern poets.

Although the poems of this period are the work of a deeply sensitive and committed artist, full of pain and longing, Bialik's outward appearance was rather different. His acquaintances knew him as a gruff, earthy, absent-minded, warm and generous man, balding and surprisingly powerful in build, with something of the air of a lapsed rabbi and a good eye for business and pretty girls. He was always very popular with children, and was an excellent teacher. He had an acid wit and a vulgar sense of humour: his upbringing among the peasants of Volhynia had left its mark.

From 1906 onwards his poetic output began to slacken as he devoted more and more time to co-editing, with Ravnitzky, the legends and folklore of the Talmud and Midrash, the *Sefer ha-Aggadah* (Book of Legends, 1908–10). His description of the meaning of legends to the Hebrew writer M. J. Berdichewsky is true of his own art as well as of his attitude to Jewish culture:

Legends are the beautiful little stones lapped by the sea for centuries and generations until they are cast up on the shore, polished and smooth. Legends pass from generation to generation. Everything superfluous falls away. What remains is the best, the most beautiful, and most worthy of keeping and remembering.[16]

While working on the *Sefer ha-Aggadah*, Bialik also experimented with other literary forms. In 1907 he wrote the first of a distinguished and highly influential series of Hebrew essays on Hebrew literature and Jewish culture in general. In 1908–9 he wrote a good deal of autobiographical fiction, including what became chapters 2–7 of *Safiaḥ* (Aftergrowth) and the short story 'Me-Aḥore ha-Gader' (Behind the Fence), telling of a friendship and, later, a sexual liaison between a Jewish boy and a Christian girl who lives next door. By now he had almost complete artistic freedom to deal with private themes which preoccupied him, including his ambivalence towards his national role. Bialik's artistic aims were not in concert with his public image. In 1909 he visited Palestine for the first time and was appalled at the rapturous welcome accorded to him as national poet. In Jaffa he tried to give a public reading of 'Me-Aḥore ha-Gader' but was stopped by the audience who wanted to hear poems of national revival and hope.

The poems of 1906–11, with the exception of a delightful group of folk poems, are filled with despair and the death-wish. Then, during the years immediately preceding the First World War, Bialik practically stopped writing poetry. His *shtika* (silence) has been the source of endless speculation. During this period he became increasingly involved with what he called *kinnus* (ingathering), a concept which, as we shall see, had particular psychological importance to him. In a landmark essay, 'Ha-Sefer ha-Ivri' (Hebrew Literature, 1913), he described *kinnus* as the collection of the fragments of Jewish culture from the countries of the Diaspora in an effort to give new force and direction to the growing Jewish national consciousness. The idea of *kinnus* was bound up with Bialik's publishing plans. In 1910 he became manager of Moriah, and from 1911 it began to expand to include all Jewish literature of value.

When the war broke out, Bialik was on holiday with his wife

in Franzensbad, Austria. Cut off, they travelled to Vienna, where Bialik was briefly arrested as an enemy national. Shortly after, they were allowed to return to Russia via Romania. Manya Bialik recalled her husband's work during the war:

> Chaim Nachman was not actually within conscription age. Men of his age [he was over forty at the outbreak of the war] who found work in a military institution or factory were not liable for conscription. Chaim Nachman found clerical work in such an institution. He would leave in the morning and come back within two or three hours.[17]

The war, the Russian revolution and the civil war which followed severely curtailed Bialik's publishing activities and virtually forced him back to writing. In July 1915 the Russian government halted the publication of Hebrew books. During the next few years, Bialik wrote a number of his most impressive poems, essays and fiction, including a new section of *Safiah*; and he also found time to do much translating and editing. Perhaps his finest essay, 'Halakhah ve-Aggadah' (Law and Legend), was written at this time. This work is memorable, among many other reasons, for its portrayal of the slow, cathedral-like growth of the Jewish tradition, generation after generation, and of the panic-stricken impulse in times of danger to save what was most valuable. The urgency which fills this essay (which was originally delivered as a speech at a Hebrew literary conference in Moscow in the winter of 1915) may be linked to the growing pressures of the war and the massive refugee problem which built up as Jews living on the western frontier of the Russian empire were forced eastward. The refugee problem seems also to have revived Bialik's memories of the effects of the 1881–4 pogroms, as reflected in his story 'Ha-Hatzotzra Nitbaysha' (The Shamed Trumpet, 1915).

After the Russian revolution of March 1917, the Jews were granted full civil rights and the ban on Hebrew was lifted. Bialik brought out the Hebrew literary anthology *Knesset*, which included a number of works which he had written during the previous two years. On 2 November 1917, five days before the Bolsheviks seized power, the British government issued the

Balfour Declaration expressing its support for a Jewish national home in Palestine (including Transjordan). The following month, British troops captured Jerusalem from the Turks, who were allied with the Germans. Bialik thought increasingly of emigration to Palestine, but remained in Odessa throughout the civil war of 1918–20. In 1918 he wrote to the Hebrew poet Avraham ben Yitzhak: 'How are we and the Russian Jews?—There is no peace! But there is much fear at the terrible times ahead—and they are sure to come.'[18]

During the next two years there were over 1000 pogroms, with an estimated 60,000 Jews murdered. Even before the consolidation of Soviet rule, the Bolsheviks in July and August 1919 issued decrees banning Zionism and liquidating all autonomous institutions of the Russian Jews. There was famine in Odessa. At this time, Manya Bialik recalled, Bialik was translating Schiller's *Wilhelm Tell* into Hebrew:

> During the Bolshevik period, when it was impossible to get essential needs, there was no light, no heat, no public services. One time I was in the kitchen and Chaim Nachman was in bed, working on his translation of *Wilhelm Tell*. Suddenly I heard a scream. I ran to him. What happened? He was sitting in bed, crying: 'I want to go to Eretz Yisrael.'[19]

Through the intercession of Maxim Gorky with Lenin, Bialik and a group of Hebrew writers obtained permission to leave Russia in 1921. 'In the name of Trotsky and Lenin,' he wrote the following year, 'they didn't leave me so much as a thread or a shoelace. I left the country with nil. I saved nothing.'[20]

Until 1924, Bialik lived mainly in Germany, where he rebuilt his publishing firm under the name Dvir. His fiftieth birthday in 1923 was celebrated throughout the Jewish world, and a special jubilee edition of his collected writings was published in Berlin. However, as always, the honour and praise which he received at this time filled him with discomfort and guilt. In 1924 he finally moved to Palestine. He built a house in Tel Aviv (today the Bialik Museum) and re-established Dvir. For the rest of his life he lived in Tel Aviv, which had become a boom town

under British rule. He was frequently abroad, as an emissary for
the Zionist Organization or for reasons of health. By this time
most of his activities were of a public nature. He was a member
of the academic board of the Hebrew University; honorary
president of the Hebrew Writers' Union; founder of the *Oneg
Shabbat* (Sabbath study programme) in Tel Aviv and of the
literary journal *Moznayim*. In 1926, at the request of Chaim
Weizmann, he spent five months in the United States on a
fund-raising mission for the Zionist Organization, accompanied
by Shmaryahu Levin, a prominent Zionist leader and a manager
of Dvir. His letters written at this time give fascinating glimpses
into his reluctant life as a public man. While crossing the
Mediterranean on the way out, for example, he wrote to
Ravnitzky: '[Levin] is my guide in English table manners: how
to hold a fork, how to eat, how to use a napkin, how to chew,
how to swallow, how to digest, how to . . . '[21] On the boat back
to Palestine, he summed up his American experience to Ahad
Ha'am:

> . . . meetings, banquets, ordinary parties, interviews,
> conversations, visits, declarations, fanfares, doctorates—
> I've been twice doctored (or donkied)—noise, tumult,
> confusion, tararum, and the usual American bluff and
> humbug . . . in the world to come they'll deduct the last
> five months from my sentence in hell.[22]

In 1931, after taking part in the Seventeenth Zionist Congress
in Basle, Bialik went on a tour of European Jewish communities
which took in thirty-three cities in eight countries and lasted
more than five months.

From the time he left Russia, Bialik's literary activity
declined, partly because of his responsibilities as a national figure.
During the 1920s, again in collaboration with Ravnitzky, he
produced the first modern critical editions of the medieval
Hebrew poets Solomon ibn Gabirol and Moses ibn Ezra.
However, the main creative work of the last quarter-century of
his life was collected shortly before his death: *Shirim u-Fizmonot
li-Ladim* (Poems and Songs for Children, 1933) and *Va-Yhi
ha-Yom* (And It Came to Pass, 1934), consisting of re-told

legends about King David and King Solomon. Because they are ostensibly meant for children, these works have been unjustly neglected by scholars. In fact they contain some of Bialik's finest work, though not on the same level of creative intensity as that of the 1903–6 period.

By the end of his life, Bialik had himself become a legendary figure. A revealing, possibly apocryphal, anecdote has him sitting in a barber shop in Tel Aviv. Two children come in. One points him out, 'That's Bialik!' and the other replies, 'Don't be silly, Bialik is a street!' For his sixtieth birthday, Manya Bialik recalled, she had to give three parties, 'One for 100 prominent members of the *yishuv*, a second for writers and artists, and a third for the Habimah company.'[23] He was so besieged by guests that he was forced to abandon his house in central Tel Aviv and move to Ramat Gan in the suburbs: 'The main advantage of having moved is that my wife and I have escaped the unwanted visitors who drove me mad and wearied my wife and me to sickness.'[24]

In Ramat Gan he wrote the only work in his *Collected Poems* which was composed in Eretz Yisrael—since moving to Tel Aviv, all his poetry had been written abroad. He completed his most ambitious poem since *Megillat ha-Esh*, the final two sections of the four-part *Yatmut* (Orphanhood, 1928, 1933, 1934). The reader has the impression that Bialik waited a lifetime to write this poem and that all his previous poetry leads up to it. It recreates the greatest trauma of the poet's life—the loss of his father and the forced separation from his mother. The contrast between the gregarious public figure and the intensely private confessional poet recalls that between the frenetic newspaper magnate in Orson Welles's film *Citizen Kane*, and the child that Kane once was, wounded to his dying breath by childhood loss. *Yatmut* might be described as Bialik's 'Rosebud', Kane's last word. The last part of the poem, 'Predah' (Separation), was written only a few weeks before Bialik's unexpected death from a heart attack in Vienna on 4 July 1934. The haunting depiction of his separation from his mother may also be read as a prophecy of his impending death.

Bialik died at the height of his fame. His death was looked

upon as a national disaster, and he was widely eulogized. As a public man, he gave the impression of being open, accessible to all and straightforward and the idea that he had a profoundly tortured buried life was not publicly recognized or desired. The poet Isaac Lamdan was more aware than most of Bialik's unseen complexities: 'Even when he was alive, we hardly knew anything about Bialik's hidden life? What do we know now?'[25]

Bialik's Epitaph

After my death say this eulogy for me:

'There was a man who died before his time,
leaving his poetry, the song of his life,
unfinished. And what a shame! he had
another song to sing, and now it's gone,
gone forever!

And what a great shame! he had a harp—
a soul expressive and alive—and the poet
used all its strings to tell his private
thoughts. But he kept one secret hidden.
Round and round his fingers played, but
one string was mute to the end, silent
to the very end.

And what a very great shame! All her days
the string quivered and strained for her song,
her redeemer. Thirsting, suffering, longing
as the heart longs for something made for it.
And though he was late in coming, she waited,
groaning in pain, but he never came,
he never came!

And the pain is so very very great! There was
a man who died before his time, leaving his
song unfinished. He had another song to sing,
and now it's gone, gone
forever!'

'Aḥare moti' (1904)

Among Jewish nationalists at the turn of the century, Bialik's spiritual, cultural and moral impact was immense; it was even comparable with that of Herzl in the political sphere. He inspired countless Russian Zionists and revolutionaries as well as two generations of *haluzim* (pioneers) in Palestine and influenced tens of thousands of schoolchildren, for even in his lifetime his poems were included in the curriculum wherever modern Hebrew was taught. He cut across political differences. Thus Jabotinsky, the moving spirit of the Jewish underground in Palestine and of Menachem Begin's Herut party in the State of Israel, regarded Bialik as his spiritual mentor. At the same time, Jabotinsky's arch-rival, Chaim Weizmann, looked upon him as an equal.[26]

Bialik's literary influence was greater than that of any other modern Hebrew writer, with the possible exception of S. J. Agnon. From the time he was thirty, when he wrote *Be-Ir ha-Haregah*, until his death, he was the centre of Hebrew literature. (It is interesting that when Bialik moved to Germany in the early 1920s, the centre shifted there, and when he arrived in Tel Aviv in 1924, the centre moved to Palestine.) As a national-cultural hero, he had no rivals. Moshe Ungerfeld, in *Bialik ve-Sofre Doro* (Bialik and the Writers of his Generation, 1974), has shown how closely Bialik was acquainted with practically all the important Hebrew writers of his day. As literary editor of *Ha-Shiloah* (1903–9), as a publisher and, above all, as a uniquely gifted artist of great ambition and integrity, Bialik set unprecedently high standards for his literary generation and after. No one equalled his achievement or seriously questioned his authority until Agnon and the poet Abraham Shlonsky arrived in Palestine in the 1920s. Bialik's writings influenced, to varying degrees, most of the Hebrew writers of his age: Agnon, Tchernichowsky, Shimoni, Shoffman, Brenner, Schneour, Gnessin, Shalom and many others. Even the aged Hebrew novelist Mendele Mokher Sefarim was influenced by Bialik in his late writings.

With the growth of the *yishuv* and, later, the establishment of the State of Israel, Bialik was gradually superseded by other, more topical writers. Yet his influence persists. Just as, in Dostoevsky's famous saying, all Russian literature came from under Gogol's 'Overcoat', so also all modern Hebrew poetry might be said to have emerged from Bialik's *Megillat ha-Esh*. There is hardly a Hebrew poet in this century who was not influenced in some way by Bialik's lyrics, though Uri Zvi Greenberg was the only one seriously to follow in Bialik's neo-prophetic style. The vast range of Bialik's experiments in rhyme and metre, which are almost totally lost in translation, opened up enormous possibilities for the future development of Hebrew poetry. Finally, his use of classical sources for the purpose of enhancing or disguising his meaning, or for the sake of irony, has also left its mark on later Hebrew poetry, notably that of Yehuda Amichai and Natan Zach. These poets would probably be the first to admit, however, that in his mastery of the sources, no poet since the creation of the Jewish state has even remotely approached Bialik.

In his lifetime, Bialik was translated into over two dozen languages. The best versions, in his view, were Jabotinsky's Russian translations, which went into seven reprints and sold tens of thousands of copies, far more than the Hebrew editions at the time.[27] Through these translations Bialik became widely known and admired among the Russian intelligentsia. Maxim Gorky hailed him as a genius, a new Isaiah, and the revolutionary poet Mayakovsky honoured him with the following lines in his poem 'The Backbone Flute':

> The vision of your bereft countenance rose;
> your eyes made it shine on the carpet
> as if some new Bialik had conjured
> a dazzling Queen of Hebrew Zion.[28]

Bialik's poems of wrath and rebellion were frequently read by Russian revolutionaries, many of whom were Jewish and had received a traditional upbringing. Manya Bialik recalled[29] that at one point the poems were regarded as so inflammatory by the Russian police that to read them in public was to risk imprisonment. When Jabotinsky gave a reading of his Russian translations, the hall was decked out to look like an engagement party, with a buffet table and a piano. Jabotinsky began to declaim and soon the audience was in tears. Suddenly the cry went up, 'Police!' The recital stopped, the piano started playing, couples began to dance... It can only be speculated what effect such poems as 'En zot, ki rabat tzerartunu' (Nothing but your fierce hounding, 1899) had on the Russian revolutionary movement:

> Nothing but your fierce hounding
> has turned us into beasts of prey.
> With cruel fury
> we'll drink your blood.
> We'll have no pity
> when the whole nation rises, cries—
> 'Revenge!'

More has been written about Bialik than about any other modern Hebrew poet: the Bialik Museum in Tel Aviv has a collection of over 30,000 such items.[30] Only a small part of the major literature on Bialik can be discussed here: a useful introduction to critical approaches is given by Samuel Werses in his *Bikoret ha-Bikoret* (Criticism of Criticism, 1982). Much of the writing on Bialik, especially in his lifetime, consisted of uncritical, fulsome praise. Words such as 'genius', 'miraculous', 'national poet', 'spokesman of the Jewish people', 'greatest Hebrew poet since Isaiah', were used so frequently that, although not unwarranted up to a point, they lost their force. Bialik's importance in the Zionist movement also had an adverse effect on the critical literature on his work, even the most overtly confessional of his lyrics being often misinterpreted as having primarily national significance. There were early exceptions, such as E. M. Lifshits and A. Avronin, but the serious study of Bialik did not get under way until after the poet's death.

Much of the criticism during the 1930s and 1940s focused on the poet's linguistic sources, textual variants in his writings, and archival material which appeared posthumously. The annual *Knesset*, an anthology of writings dedicated to Bialik's memory (1934–46), gave much impetus to the criticism of his writings. An important element in the development of Bialik criticism was the publication in 1935 of his speeches and, in 1937–9, of about 1500 of his letters. These and, later, Lachower's biography, which came out between 1944 and 1948, made possible reasonably authoritative literary-biographical studies. Unfortunately, much of this work is badly in need of revision, and practically none of it has been translated into English.

All the most influential Hebrew critics since the war have written on Bialik. Joseph Klausner has emphasized the historical-biographical basis of Bialik's writings. Dov Sadan and Adi Zemach, among others, have made close studies of his recurrent use of symbols, such as the cloud, the lit candle or the broken fence. Baruch Kurzweil, perhaps the most sensitive and perceptive of Bialik's critics, has stressed that he was the great poet of the crisis of faith caused by the momentous transition among the eastern European Jews from an entirely religious way of life to an increasingly secular-nationalist outlook. Recent studies by Dan Miron and Ziva Shamir have focused on Bialik's complex relationship to his role as national poet. All these approaches and others have built up a coherent picture of the man and his achievement.

Nevertheless, critical work on Bialik leaves much to be desired. One of the main shortcomings is that critics tend to focus on a part or parts of Bialik's works, and an overview is lacking. In addition, a crucial element in Bialik's writings has been largely neglected: the remarkable interconnection of specific elements in his personal life with his role as national poet. Finally, and not least, there is no full-length critical or biographical work on Bialik in English. The present work sets out, among other things, to remedy these shortcomings.

2

THE BACKGROUND

The life and works of Bialik represent an extraordinary, perhaps unique, convergence of social and historical currents, many of them conflicting and most of them foreign to the modern reader. It is vital to begin by discussing these individually. The forces which made Bialik include: the Russian Pale of Settlement, the educational system which prevailed among the European Jews, Hasidism, the Enlightenment (*Haskalah*), Romanticism, Nationalism, anti-Semitism and Zionism. Bialik's achievement as a poet lies in the fact that, although he was deeply affected by each of these forces, he mastered and used them in the service of his own distinctive art.

Bialik spent most of his early life in Volhynia, in the heart of the so-called Pale of Settlement.[1] Perhaps the single most important fact to bear in mind about the Russian Jews is that they had come under Russian rule with the partitions of Poland in the late eighteenth century. For about three centuries previously, the Jews had not been allowed to live in the Russian interior, and the Pale was a large reservation on the western frontier of the Russian empire where the Jews were confined, increasingly impoverished and overcrowded, until the March 1917 revolution. At the time of the partitions the Polish Jews were the most homogeneous and numerous of all European Jewish communities, comprising about one million, which at that time was about one-third of the world's Jewish population. By the end of the nineteenth century, their numbers had swelled to five million. Conditions in the Pale were always poor, but they worsened in the course of the century.

Russia's own insuperable difficulties in adapting to the rapidly changing modern world and in controlling its vast, heterogeneous population were reflected in its treatment of the Jews. Had they been allowed and able to adapt smoothly to Russian society, it is highly unlikely that a Jewish national movement and accompanying modern Hebrew culture would have developed there. The rise of Zionism and Hebrew was bound up with the instability of Tsarist rule and the decline and fall of the Romanovs. To understand why Bialik became a Hebrew, rather than a Russian, poet, it is useful to sketch in the background to the Jews' general failure to assimilate into Russian society in the course of the nineteenth century.

The Jews had come under Russian rule in unfavourable conditions. Poland had been periodically at war with Russia during the two centuries before the partitions and the Polish Jews naturally sided with Poland. Their social and economic position under Polish rule was unstable, but tolerable on the whole, and their religious life was intensely rich. They had almost complete control over their internal affairs. Russia's power struggle with Poland had left deep hatred and suspicion among the Polish Jews. In 1648–9 the Russian Cossacks, led by Bogdan Khmelnitsky, had carried out the largest massacres of Jews before Hitler. After the partitions of Poland the Jews who came under Russian rule were not unsympathetic to Polish nationalism, and were suspected by the Russians of being potential traitors. This suspicion is reflected in Russian literature, for example in Turgenev's story 'The Jew', Gogol's novel *Taras Bulba*, and in the writings of Pushkin, Dostoevsky and even Tolstoy. Following the Polish insurrection of 1863, there was an anti-Semitic backlash in Russia.

A second, far more important, reason why the Jews were not easily assimilated into Russian society was the traditional hatred of the Jews taught by the Russian Orthodox Church. The Jews were popularly regarded as the killers of Christ, a parasitical, potentially dangerous group which could be used or abused with impunity. Religious and political hatred merged as the Jews, some of whom had been Polish patriots, were seen as new Judases. Anti-Semitism had been responsible for the ban on Jews in the Russian interior before the partitions of Poland, and there was no intention of changing this policy. Russian policy towards the Jews, as towards all other groups in the empire, was inevitably one of pure expedience, consistent above all in the desire to preserve the status quo. The government feared that the spread of the Jews would undermine the economy and provoke anti-authoritarian dissidence among the indigenous population. By laws of 1795 and 1835, the Jews were confined within the Pale, denied, unlike other groups, the right to move freely within Russia. Their assimilation into Russian society was further hampered by the dozens of anti-Semitic laws passed against them, especially during the tyrannous reign of Nicholas I. Throughout the first half of the nineteenth century, it was government policy to encourage and in some cases to force the Jews to convert to Christianity.

Integration was further inhibited by the Jews' own unwillingness to be 'Russified'. Their general attitude towards the Russian government was one of almost unmitigated loathing and distrust. They were alienated by the anti-Semitic legislation and in addition, for all their backwardness, the Jews were educated in comparison with the overwhelming majority of Russians, who were illiterate peasants. Until well into the nineteenth century, Russia had relatively little distinctive intellectual culture. As late as 1846, the Russian critic Nikolai Chernyshevsky could write: 'What have the Russians given to learning? Alas, nothing. What has learning contributed to Russian life? Again, nothing.'[2] This view, and similar ones, is echoed in the writings of Belinsky, Chaadaev and others. In contrast, the Jews had an ancient religious culture and educational tradition which were of the utmost importance in preserving the unity and morale of the Russian Jews. Proud of their heritage, they had little interest in the peasant life around them, or in the dozens of languages with which they came into contact. They preserved their way of life and their languages—Yiddish for everyday, Hebrew for prayer and study. A hundred years after the partitions of Poland, most of the Russian Jews could not communicate properly with their Christian neighbours: in the 1897 census, 97 per cent gave Yiddish as their main language.

The Jewish educational tradition formed an integral part of the background to Bialik's emergence as a Hebrew poet and Jewish national figure. His education was essentially no different from that of most European Jews, particularly in the Pale of Settlement, and his lifelong preoccupation with education was instilled in him in childhood.

Before the introduction of compulsory education in Europe in the late nineteenth and early twentieth centuries, only two large European groups were literate: the priests and the Jews. The educational tradition, which is central to Judaism, had its roots in Palestine in the late-biblical and early Talmudic periods. In Europe, Jewish education evolved into a three-part system, the *ḥeder, bet midrash* and yeshivah, each part of which Bialik experienced and wrote about. He described these as 'the strongest fortresses in our long, hard struggle for survival, for our right to exist as a separate and unique people among the nations'.[3]

In each of these institutions, the Scriptures were treated as the word of God. The secular study of Jewish literature was almost unknown before the twentieth century. Bialik's first and most lasting impressions of Hebrew were of the Holy Tongue. The immense care with which he wrote later in life was a sign of his reverence for the language which he had learned in childhood. For much of the early part of his career, Bialik was in the shadow of the Scriptures, struggling to emerge as a poet with an original voice of his own.

The *ḥeder* (or 'room', where classes were held) was for children up to the age of thirteen. The main subject of study was the Five Books of Moses (the Chumash) with the commentary of the eleventh-century exegete Rashi. Unfortunately, *ḥeder* teachers were often bitterly frustrated men who vented their anger on their charges. Bialik's first teacher was 'a vulgar boor: curses and blows—that was his Torah'.[4] Afterwards he moved to another *ḥeder*, where he was treated kindly and his imagination was allowed to develop. He writes in *Safiaḥ* that the study of the Scriptures was a revelation of the world around him:

The gate of understanding opened of its own accord: 'As a tree planted' [Ps. 1 : 3] obviously could only mean the tree in whose shadow we were sitting; 'by streams of water' could only mean the pool of water down in the valley. 'The valley of the shadow' [Ps. 23:4] must be the ruin where the evil spirits were to be found, and which our teacher would never let us approach. 'Thou preparest a table before me' could be none other than the table at which we were sitting and engaging in the Lord's own Torah.[5]

Other memories, of private study in his grandparents' home and in the local *bet midrash* (house of study) in Zhitomir, are also described vividly by Bialik. In his grandparents' house, as we have seen, he was bored and oppressed by the excess of learning, which was equated with morality, and by the entire religious way of life.[6] For about four years, from the age of thirteen, he studied alone in the *bet midrash*, traditionally used both for study and prayer by older children and adults. Bialik soon gained a reputation as an *iluy* (prodigy) in Talmud. The wild, undisciplined child had become a respected scholar who was consulted on questions of Jewish law.[7] In several of his poems, Bialik used the house of study as a symbol of a once powerful tradition which had declined.

From May 1890 until September 1891, Bialik was a student at the Volozhin yeshivah. During part of this time he lived as a genuine *matmid* (a day-and-night Talmud student), absorbing himself body and soul in the study of the Torah. His poem *Ha-Matmid* is based largely on these experiences. Perhaps no artist has ever conveyed so well the sheer passion for learning which has traditionally been part of Jewish life:

> Lord, take what you will—my flesh and blood—
> I swear by your holy Torah, if I sleep . . .
> Before I slake my thirst for your Word.

The *matmid* continues the age-old tradition of learning the Torah, but in the process denies himself the enjoyment of life's pleasures. Like many of Bialik's early poems, this poem has too much overflowing sentiment for modern taste, though it is utterly sincere and has moments of power. Its central theme—

self-denial in the interest of a higher ideal—recurs in his later life and writings.

Bialik's character, role and impact were strongly conditioned by the Hasidic milieu into which he was born. His birthplace, Volhynia in the Ukraine, a mostly backward, rural area where ignorance and superstition abounded, was the heartland of Hasidism. The movement was founded by the legendary Rabbi Israel ben Eliezer, known as the Ba'al Shem Tov ('Master of the Good Name [of God]', 1700?–60). It began in reaction to the dry, melancholy scholasticism which prevailed in European Jewish communities following the 1648–9 massacres and the crushing of popular messianic hopes after Shabbetai Zvi (1627–76), who was widely believed by the Jews to be the Messiah, converted to Islam in 1670. Hasidism drew much of its inspiration and ideas from Jewish mysticism, or Kabbalah. It attached the highest importance to joyful prayer, rather than study, in the attempt to attain unity (*devekut*) with God.[8]

Hasidism is generally regarded as the most important Jewish religious movement since the destruction of the Temple in Jerusalem in 70 CE. It spoke so directly to the needs of the Jewish masses that by the end of the eighteenth century about half the Jews in eastern Europe were *hasidim*. At this time and for the next two generations, the movement was severely attacked, notably by Rabbi Elijah ben Solomon Zalman, known as the Vilna Gaon (1720–97). Its opponents, who were in favour of a more rational, intellectual brand of Judaism, became known as the *mitnagdim* ('adversaries'). However, by the mid-nineteenth century, the animosity between *hasidim* and *mitnagdim* had died down: the *hasidim* had become more conservative and the two groups now had a common foe—the Enlightenment (*Haskalah*). The growth of the yeshivah movement in the latter part of the nineteenth century was, to a large extent, a reaction to Enlightenment, a means of protecting the young from assimilation. By the end of the century it was possible for a Hasidic boy such as Bialik to study in one of the former bastions of the *mitnagdim*, the yeshivah of Volozhin, which had been founded by a pupil of the Vilna Gaon, Chaim of Volozhin (1749–1821), who had made one of the most profound, systematic and scholarly attacks on Hasidism in his book *Nefesh ha-Hayyim* (The Soul of Life, 1824).

In his maturity, Bialik himself had little sympathy for the cult of personality which was (and still is) a central feature of Hasidism and which was frequently attacked by the *mitnagdim*. Nevertheless, the popular reaction to him (like his own reaction to Ahad Ha'am in the 1890s) had certain limited elements in common with the response of the eastern European Jews to their charismatic wonder rabbis, the quacks, exorcists and faith healers, who were often believed to be omnipotent and omniscient, and who also, at times, possessed outstanding qualities of leadership and spiritual teachings. The uncritical adulation to which Bialik was subjected in his lifetime—and which he found burdensome—recalls the unswerving devotion of the *hasidim* to their *rebbe*, who in their eyes could do no wrong. At times, Bialik was even associated with almost supernatural powers. After his death, for example, a rumour arose that his watch had stopped at the precise moment of his passing: exactly the same sort of tale was common in Hasidic legends.

A number of salient qualities in Bialik's writings may be traced to his Hasidic origins. There is his emphasis on the joy of the natural world as a source of spiritual insight. There is the *hitlahavut* (devotional enthusiasm) with which he depicts Jewish national institutions and hopes. There is also the semi-erotic depiction of religious experience, and the use of religious imagery to describe erotic experience, both of which are familiar in Hasidic and Kabbalistic literature. The idea that good and evil are inseparably bound up with one another, in *Megillat ha-Esh* for example, is also reminiscent of Hasidic teachings. The language and imagery adopted by the *hasidim*, such as *zohar* (radiance), *devekut* (cleaving to God), *shevirat ha-kelim* (the breaking of the vessels), *nitzotzot* (sparks of holiness), appear frequently in Bialik's writings. Yet, as a 'Zionist *rebbe*', Bialik offered little of the religious faith of the Hasidic masters, and his faith in Zionism was far from absolute. In his poems of pessimism, despair and death, Bialik expressed a spirit largely antithetical to Hasidism.

At the same time that Hasidism was sweeping across eastern Europe, in the late eighteenth century, the Enlightenment (or *Aufklärung*) was profoundly changing the face of the western European Jewish communities. The creation of Hebrew as an instrument of secular communication and art was largely brought about by the Enlightenment, and Bialik's works, the poet readily admitted, could not have been written without it.[9] The *Haskalah* and its relation to Jewish tradition is an important theme in Bialik's early writings; in his poetry it is symbolized by light.

The process of the Enlightenment among the Jews began with the dominant figure of the German-Jewish philosopher Moses Mendelssohn (1729–86). The German Jews of the mid-eighteenth century had led a traditional, insular life in the ghettos, largely ignorant of German and of the modern world. The movement began with the premise that the Jews were socially and educationally inferior to the enlightened Western minority, that their way of life must be broken down and modified in order for them to gain acceptance and civil rights in the gentile world. The *Haskalah* was largely a mirror of liberal gentile attitudes towards the Jews. Yiddish, the language of the vast majority of the European Jews, was unacceptable as a catalyst for *Haskalah* ideals of reform and education. It was despised as a hybrid language, the language of the ghetto, holding the Jews back from entering Western civilization. Hebrew, in contrast, was a highly esteemed classical language, taught in all respectable universities.

Mendelssohn was the first to conceive of Hebrew as a bridge enabling the Jews to cross from the ghetto into the modern world. He was responsible for translating the Pentateuch into German (with a Hebrew commentary) and started the first modern Hebrew journal, *Ha-Me'asef* (The Gatherer). This work was enormously successful. By encouraging the German Jews to learn German via Hebrew, Mendelssohn was able to introduce them to the ideas of the Enlightenment. The rising German-Jewish middle class found support and confidence in the new ideology, with its emphasis on 'reason', 'good taste' and 'the rights of man'. Hebrew literature of this period was mostly stilted and propagandistic, yet it did prove that the language was capable of being adapted to modern, secular purposes. By the end of the eighteenth century, the use of Hebrew petered out in Germany as it was no longer needed: the German Jews had learned German, and they had become largely assimilated into German society. The *Haskalah* movement, spurred on by the liberal spirit of the age following the French revolution, took root in other European centres: by the 1820s it reached the Russian Pale of Settlement.

The nature of the Russian *Haskalah* movement—the relationship of the *Maskilim* (exponents of the *Haskalah*) to their fellow Russian Jews, the government's attitude towards the *Haskalah*, and vice versa—was fraught with ambivalence, complexity and inconsistency. It is an extraordinary irony, in the light of future events, that the Tsarist government, while pursuing openly anti-Semitic policies, originally allowed, encouraged and even subsidized Hebrew literature. There was good reason for this. The government looked upon Hebrew as a potentially valuable tool of education, reform and Russian patriotism, and also as a means of breaking down the religious and social defences which protected the Jews from assimilation and, ultimately, conversion. The example of the German Jews was not lost on the Russian intelligentsia.

However, the circumstances of the Russian Jews were far different from those in Western Europe. They were far more numerous and lived mostly in rural areas; hardly any of the Russian Jews were professionally trained; most were desperately poor. Deeply attached to their religious tradition, they were exposed to no significant secular civilization, such as that of the Germans, which they wished to emulate. They also suffered far more anti-Semitic oppression than their Western brethren. The deep suspicion of the Russian Jews towards government efforts to educate them is illustrated by the fact that in 1853 there were only 159 Jewish students in the Russian secondary school system.

Only after the accession of Alexander II in 1855 did the *Haskalah* begin to have an appreciable effect on the Russian Jews. The disastrous Crimean War had exposed Russia's backwardness and the dire need for change. Under the pressure for reform, the government gradually allowed professionally trained Jews—a tiny minority—to move into the interior. This and other reforms, most importantly the freeing of the serfs in 1861, created an optimistic spirit among the Russian Jews. There were hopes that civil rights and emancipation were not long in coming. For the first time, they began to send their children to schools (as opposed to *ḥeders*) in substantial numbers. Within a generation, Jewish schoolchildren and university students were represented out of all proportion to the numbers of the Russian Jews, and the government imposed a quota, but in the 1850s and 1860s the Russian *Haskalah* had its heyday. Hebrew fiction and poetry flourished, together with drama, autobiography, translation and various other types of literature. The modern Hebrew (and Yiddish) press effectively began during this period. Much of this literature was saturated with propaganda, criticisms of traditional Judaism, even a measure of self-hate. In part this modern writing turned upon itself because censorship made impossible open criticism of Russian anti-Semitism and of the existence of the Pale. Virtually none of this literature was of permanent artistic value, but its historical importance was immense.

As in Germany, the educated Russian Jews became assimilated and largely alienated from traditional Judaism, and by the 1870s Hebrew had declined. The trend to assimilation would probably have continued if not for the growing anti-Semitism in Russia following the Polish revolt of 1863 and culminating in the pogroms of 1881–4. The pogroms exploded all lingering hopes among the Russian Jewish intellectuals that Enlightenment would bring them emancipation. The *Haskalah* and the use of Hebrew as a tool of the *Haskalah* came violently and suddenly to an end.

The Tsarist government, which always had the power to ban or suppress Hebrew, allowed it to flourish for reasons which varied at different times from crude anti-Semitism to enlightened liberalism. It underestimated the power of the language, for it did not anticipate that Hebrew could be a latent force of Jewish nationalism, not merely a tool of 'Russification'. Accidentally, therefore, with the rise of Jewish nationalism in the 1880s,

Hebrew evolved from being an educational tool to an integral part of Jewish nationalism. The *Haskalah* inadvertently prepared the ground for the rise of Hebrew and gave Bialik the springboard he needed to become a national poet. Precisely at the moment when Hebrew became a part of the Jewish national renaissance, Hebrew writers began to produce works of enduring art.

In common with Hasidism, Romanticism was one of a number of eighteenth-century movements which sprang up in various parts of Europe, seemingly unconnected with one another but with much in common: the protest against artificially binding forms of worship, custom and government; the advocacy of free, sincere, spontaneous, even overflowing self-expression; the quest for nature and the attempt to heighten the powers of the individual in the natural world; the glorification of an almost superhuman figure. All these major characteristics of Romanticism are found in Bialik's poetry.[10]

By virtue of a time-lag which affected Hebrew literature generally, Bialik was influenced far less by contemporary trends than by early nineteenth-century literature, by the German and Russian Romantics in particular. Like the great Romantics, Bialik was himself one of the chief subjects of his poetry, most strikingly in his poetry of childhood. From his earliest experiments in verse he drew heavily on Romantic imagery of pools, light, clouds, woods, the sky, the changing seasons, to express states of mind, and by 1905 he had raised Hebrew Romanticism to a creative level comparable in its beauty, intelligence, sensitivity and technique to the poetry of Wordsworth, Schiller and the young Pushkin.

The tension between egoistic introspection and the wish to be absorbed in some sort of One, which Friedrich Schlegel, one of the leading philosophers and literary critics of the Enlightenment, regarded as a central quality of Romanticism, is found repeatedly in Bialik's writings. This tension was caused in no small measure by his role as national poet. This national role may be linked with the Romantic movement in a number of other ways as well. For Zionism, with its roots in the Bible, was originally a form of Romanticism and far closer to poetry than it is today. The longing for a heroic past, for something lost, for a distant land, for the glory of a bygone age, and the attempt to dignify the unfortunate and the downtrodden, are common to both movements. The neo-biblical Romantic spirit which animated English, Greek, Polish and Italian nationalism also gave Jewish nationalism the breath of life. The Romantic idea, expressed by poets such as Byron and Shelley, that poets can change the world, are indeed 'the unacknowledged legislators of mankind', reaches its consummation in the life and work of Bialik. The early Romantics may have idealized the Wandering Jew, sympathizing with his plight and with his dream of the return to Zion: Bialik helped to make the dream real.

Bialik's rise as a Hebrew artist in Russia would hardly have been as spectacular as it was without the Zionist movement. The rise of Jewish nationalism, in turn, would have been extremely unlikely if not for two powerful, interconnected nineteenth-century European phenomena: nationalism and anti-Semitism. Bialik's role as national poet is linked to the general context of European nationalism. Modern nationalism—the idea that a people is a separate entity, the indivisible master of its fate, owing allegiance to no power, possessing unique characteristics, with common bonds uniting its citizens—was born with the French revolution. The Napoleonic wars greatly stimulated among European peoples the awareness of their differences and set off movements of national liberation or unity throughout Europe. Greece attained independence in 1832, Italy was united in 1866, Germany in 1871. In addition, from the late eighteenth century, another type of nationalism arose in Poland. The historian J. L. Talmon has described Polish nationalism as 'Judaic', 'that of a conquered humiliated and oppressed nation dreaming of resurrection'.[11] Polish nationalism, directly or indirectly, affected the fate of the Russian Jews and the rise of Jewish nationalism.

The phenomenon of national sentiment divorced from territorial government, as in Poland, was given tremendous impetus, especially among the Slavs, by the work of Johann Gottfried Herder (1744–1803). Herder, a Prussian who lived in

Riga, taught that every tribe or people was unfathomably and indestructibly unique. This uniqueness was based on history, cultural heritage, language and folklore. The late nineteenth-century identification of the Jews as a nation with a unique culture, language and territory was influenced partly by Herder. (This idea was first put forward with cogency and emphasis by Peretz Smolenskin [1842?–1884], a Russian who lived in Vienna and edited the leading Hebrew journal of the generation before Bialik, *Ha-Shahar* [The Dawn].) The importance which Bialik attached to folklore may also be traced to Herder's influence. For Bialik spent more time on the *Sefer ha-Aggadah* than on any of his other works; during the years 1918–22, he edited *Reshumot*, a journal of Jewish folklore; he wrote the first folk poems in Hebrew; and his writings are rich in allusions to *aggadah*.

European nationalism provided a variety of models for the evolution of Jewish nationalism. Equally important, if not more so, was the increase in anti-Semitism in the course of the nineteenth century. For nationalist sentiment often led to the distrust and exclusion of minorities, the Jews in particular.

Many of Bialik's poems, most strikingly those written during the 1903–6 period, were triggered off or affected indirectly by anti-Semitic outrages:[12] his writings, and Hebrew literature generally, might be seen as a reaction to the Russian maltreatment of the Jews. On one level, Hebrew literature was a declaration of independence: 'We Jews are blatantly discriminated against in Russia. Why should we aim to integrate ourselves into a society which hates us? We have a history, language and land of our own, of which we are proud!'

Many of the elements of Nazi anti-Jewish ordinances of the 1930s were anticipated in some form under Tsarist rule: the confinement of the Jews in a restricted space; the dozens of discriminatory laws (many of which went against Russia's own interest); the breaking up of families and the transports of children in inhuman conditions (during the reign of Nicholas I); the humiliations, the proliferation of anti-Semitic propaganda (the forgery *The Protocols of the Elders of Zion* was a Russian product); the accusations that the Jews were an alien element invading Russian life, gaining control of the press and the government, corrupting Russian culture and generally acting as a destructive force. Most sinister of all was the attempt, which began under Nicholas I, to divide the Jews into 'useful' and 'non-useful', and the manifesto of the early twentieth-century group the Black Hundreds (of which the Tsar was an honorary member), calling for the extermination of the Jews.

The increase in Russian anti-Semitism in the course of the nineteenth century was a reflection of government failure to adapt to the pressures for change which built up after the Crimean War and the freeing of the serfs in 1861. Russian anti-Semitism was a political tool used to divert general dissatisfaction with the government and revolutionary unrest on to the Jews. The freeing of the serfs, over 30 million of whom lived in the Pale, caused enormous problems there. Poverty, overcrowding and tension increased. At this time, Russia had the highest population growth in Europe—and the lowest grain yields. As anti-Semitism rose among the peasants, it also grew among the Russian intelligentsia who resented and felt threatened by the success of the Jewish assimilationists. The first pogrom, an adumbration of things to come, broke out in Odessa in 1871. Russian nationalism, stirred up by the Polish revolt of 1863 and by the Balkan War of 1877–8, also had the effect of rousing hatred for the Jews.

The turning point was reached with the assassination of Tsar Alexander II by revolutionaries on 13 March 1881. This act led to the first of three major waves of pogroms, and changed the entire course of modern Jewish history. For the next eighteen months anti-Jewish riots broke out, with tacit government consent, in over 150 towns in the Pale. In the official investigation the Jews were found to be guilty of 'exploiting' the peasants, provoking the violence, and they were subjected to laws (the 'May Laws', passed in May 1882) which, in effect, constricted the Pale and restricted still further their movements and livelihoods.

Bialik's story 'Ha-Hatzotzra Nitbaysha' describes a typically cruel incident of the times: a Jewish family about to celebrate Passover are informed by government officials that they must move elsewhere. And indeed, the Jews had no choice but to move. It is estimated that during the 1880s a million and a half Jews living in rural areas, on the western frontier or east of the Pale, were forced to move into the towns of the Pale. As a child, Bialik was an eyewitness to the effects of these upheavals. At this time, the mass migration of over two million of the Russian Jews began. Most went to America, but a small number came to Palestine where they formed the nucleus of the *yishuv*. Within Russia, an increasing number of young Jews joined the socialist or revolutionary movements.

The second wave of pogroms, in 1903–6, provoked some of Bialik's greatest poems, including *Be-Ir ha-Haregah*. By this time, approximately half of those sentenced for political offences in Russia were Jews. The Russan defeat by the Japanese in the Far East and the general strike of 1905 brought Russia to the brink of revolution. In October 1905 Tsar Nicholas II capitulated by granting a constitutional government with a legislature (Duma). Immediately, pogroms broke out in over 600 towns and villages in southern Russia. In one week about 900 Jews were murdered and over 8000 injured. Bialik was in Odessa, the scene of one of the bloodiest of the pogroms.

The third, and most brutal, wave of pogroms took place during the Russian civil war, in 1918–20. In its wake Bialik made his decision to move to Palestine.

Modern Zionism, inspired by the age-old longing of the Jews to return to the Land of Israel, effectively began with the pogroms of 1881 and the May Laws.[13] Jewish intellectuals who, during the period of reforms in the 1850s and 1860s had been fiercely patriotic, had trusted in the good intentions of the Tsar and hoped for reform through education and social change, now abandoned their patriotism, their trust and hopes. Leon Pinsker (1821–91), by training a doctor, was one of these. In his famous treatise 'Autoemancipation', published in Berlin in 1882, he offered, in effect, a diagnosis of the ailments of the Jews and argued that the Jews had no cure but to take their fate into their own hands. Pinsker was one of the founders of the Ḥibbat Zion movement in Odessa, which helped bring, settle and support the first wave (*aliyah*) of modern Jewish immigrants to Palestine, then under Turkish rule. Some 25,000 Russian Jews arrived in Palestine by the turn of the century. Many of Bialik's early poems touch on the poet's bitter alienation from Russia and his admiration for the pioneers in Palestine.

Like the creation of the *Ḥibbat Zion* movement, the founding of the Zionist Organization by Herzl in 1897 was in direct response to anti-Semitism, for Herzl first became convinced of the need for a Jewish state as a correspondent at the trial of Alfred Dreyfus in Paris in 1895. By this time there were several hundred Zionist societies in Russia, and a growing number of Hebrew readers and speakers. The Zionist Congress in Basle was greeted with almost messianic hopes by the Russian Jews. It is interesting, however, that Bialik's initial response to Herzl was the satire 'Rabi Zaraḥ', which attacked Herzl as another in a long line of false Messiahs (and which Ahad Ha'am, then editor of the newly founded *Ha-Shiloaḥ*, refused to print).[14] However, the seriousness of the Zionist enterprise soon became apparent to him. A few of his best-known poems captured the spirit of Zionism in its early, heroic and starry-eyed days: others show that his optimism was not unmixed with doubts and even despair.

By the time of the Kishinev pogrom in 1903, the Zionist Organization had found its main grass roots support in the Pale of Settlement. With over 1500 Zionist societies, the Russian Jews were by far the largest group in the movement. Their identification with Zionism was a gauge of their insecurity in Russia. Like the first wave of pogroms in 1881, the second outbreak set off a wave of *aliyah* which lasted until the start of the First World War. During this time about 40,000 highly motivated Jewish immigrants, mostly Russian, entered Turkish Palestine.

The pogroms and the general conditions in the Pale forced the Jews to become far more autonomous than they would otherwise have been. This self-sufficiency, which is reflected in Hebrew art, was transplanted to Palestine. For example, the pogroms forced the Jews to form self-defence groups, the first of which fought during the pogrom in Gomel in September 1903. (One source of inspiration for these groups was Bialik's *Be-Ir ha-Haregah*.) Many of these fighters later came to Palestine where they formed the nucleus of the Haganah, later the Israel Defence Force.

Similarly, the Jews had to suppport their own social services. It is estimated that by the end of the century, as many as 40 per cent of the Russian Jews, pauperized by unemployment and government discrimination, were living off some form or another of Jewish charity. The Bund, the first union of Jewish workers in Russia, was founded in 1897. The spirit of mutual aid in the interest of survival was transferred to Palestine as well as to other centres of Russian Jewish immigration, mainly the United States.

Until 1917, Russia remained the heartland of Zionism. Following the revolution, the Balfour Declaration, the British conquest of Palestine, and the ban on Zionism in Russia, the centre shifted to Palestine. The third wave of Russian pogroms, in 1918–20, set off the third *aliyah* which lasted until 1923 and brought an additional 35,000 Jews to Palestine. Through a mixture of diplomacy, violence, hard work and accident, the foundations were laid which later became the State of Israel.

Among the salient features of Jewish nationalism was the degree to which it found inspiration and justification in traditional Jewish sources, the Bible and prayer book in particular. In common with many of his generation, Bialik was not strictly observant,[15] yet his secular Zionism derived from a deep religious love for the land of Israel and the Hebrew language, as taught in traditional Jewish literature.

He transformed these sources into the elements of secular art, a transformation which may be seen as an emblem of the transition of the Jewish people from the world of the *shtetl* into the modern world. Bialik was the first modern Hebrew poet successfully to harness traditional Jewish literature in the service of individual self-expression. It may be that Bialik was himself uncertain whether his art was a revolutionary heresy or a continuation of the tradition. The guilt and despair in his poetry spring in part from his feeling that he had abandoned the faith, yet it may be that to the artist, who follows or creates his own inner rules, the concepts of 'heresy' or 'tradition' are irrelevant.

In the Mishna (*Berakhot*, ch. 9), the 'heretics' (in this case the Sadducees) are reported as denying the existence of the world to come—'There is but one world.' In the poem 'Yam ha-demamah polet sodot' (The sea of quiet spits secrets, 1901), the poet recasts this source in relation to his own art. He negates not just the world to come but also this world. To the poet, there is only one reality:

> One world alone is mine—
> The one in my heart.

3

LITERARY ROOTS

Bialik's poetic style at its best recalls the Bible or Shakespeare in its rich intensity, the power of its invention, its hypnotic rhythm and music. It demands a knowledge of Jewish sources, which very few readers possess today. His Hebrew readership from the 1890s until his death consisted largely of Russian Jews who, in childhood at least, had been steeped in the Scriptures and the Talmud, and to whom allusions to these sources were natural and exciting. In the poem 'Aḥare moti', quoted in Chapter 1, the following allusions, among others, would have been called up in the minds of many of Bialik's readers, and opened up whole vistas of interpretation:

> O God, thou art my God, I seek thee,
> my soul thirsts for thee;
> my flesh faints for thee . . .
>
> > (Psalms 63 : 1)

> 'Go, go'—we say to the Nazirite—'round and round,
> you will not reach the vineyard.'
>
> > (*Shabbat* 13a)

> The twelfth principle—the days after the Messiah
> comes, that is to say, we should believe
> that he will come in time, 'If he tarries—
> wait for him'   (Habbakuk 2: 3)
> > Maimonides, The Thirteen Principles of Faith,
> > from the *Mishne Torah*

Bialik's language was based almost entirely on literary, rather than colloquial, Hebrew. As late as 1910 it was still unclear whether spoken Hebrew would be successfully revived in Palestine. (The Jewish population there was under 100,000 and the schoolteachers in the Jewish schools had not yet fully succeeded in their momentous struggle to make Hebrew the sole language of instruction.) That year, while working on a series of folk poems, Bialik wrote to a colleague how extraordinary it was that these poems were being written in a language that was not generally spoken.[1] He himself spoke Yiddish at home, Russian and Yiddish with his fellow writers, and did not normally speak everyday Hebrew (though he did teach and lecture in Hebrew) until he came to Palestine in 1924. Even then, he used it somewhat reluctantly, as the following, possibly apocryphal, story reveals. Gershom Scholem, the founder of the study of Jewish mysticism, was a protégé of Bialik's. Scholem, a punctilious German, insisted on speaking Hebrew at every opportunity. Once, in Tel Aviv, Bialik was speaking in Yiddish with some literary companions when he spied Scholem on his way to see him. 'Do kommt der yekke,' he said. 'Man darf redn loshn koydesh.' ('Here comes that German. We've got to speak the Holy Tongue.')

Bialik was the first modern Hebrew poet to harness the sources and create a subtle, harmonious style in which, in his finest poems, each line is distinctly his own.[2] The advance in his poetry over that of the *Haskalah* is comparable with that of Chaucer over John Gower in fourteenth-century English poetry. How did he make this great leap forward?

Bialik's secret lay in his use of the full linguistic richness of Hebrew (and, to a lesser extent, of Aramaic, its sister language), particularly the *aggadah*. Not that *Haskalah* poets such as Judah Leib Gordon were ignorant of the Talmud. But they were inhibited by the circumstances in which they wrote and by their own anti-clerical propaganda. They tended to accept the prevailing government view of the Talmud as a source of Jewish backwardness and insularity and a bar to Russification. (At one point, in the 1830s, the Talmud was publicly burned in Russia.) In Gordon's best-known poems, for example, there are relatively few allusions to the Talmud and a vast number of biblical allusions. The references to the Talmud are usually presented in a derogatory or critical manner. Bialik, in contrast, was positively promiscuous in the use of all the linguistic and technical means at his disposal to achieve his aim of creating as perfect a work of art as possible. Some idea of his use of the sources and the nature of the literary influences on him may be obtained by looking at these individually.

The Bible. Bialik regarded the Bible as a substitute homeland for the Jews of the dispersion, the quintessence of spiritual power for all generations.[3] His debt to the Bible was immense, as A. Avital has shown in *Shirat Bialik veha-Tanach* (Bialik's Poetry and the Bible, 1951). This is a full-length book, by no means comprehensive, giving the biblical quotations drawn on by Bialik in several dozen of his poems. However, Bialik's use of the Bible usually involved some linguistic or contextual change, with the result that the reader is often unaware of, or caught off balance by, the borrowing. 'The good poet imitates,' wrote T. S. Eliot. 'The great poet steals.'

In the early poems the borrowing is rather more blatant than in the later poems, and is not infrequently reminiscent of the *Haskalah* style. In 'Hirhure Laila' (Night Meditations, 1894), the poet addresses his muse—he was only twenty-one when he wrote the poem—and asks for a bottle to hold his reader's tears, tears which he will arouse with his poems of Zion's ruin. The imagery is taken from the Psalms, but detached from its original theological context, for the psalmist is addressing God:

> Thou hast kept count of my turnings;
> put thou my tears in thy bottle!
> Are they not in thy book?   (56: 8)

Similarly, in his use of Isaiah in the poem 'Akhen ḥatzir ha-am'—'Surely the people is grass, dry as a tree'—Bialik recasts his source. Isaiah's message is that men die as grass dies, but the word of God is eternal:

> The grass withers, the flower fades,
> when the breath of the Lord blows upon it;
> surely the people is grass.   (40: 7)

The line 'surely the people is grass' is changed by Bialik into a terrible reproach: the Jewish people are incapable of being revived, they are weak and passive as grass.

As he achieved greater mastery of the biblical style, Bialik used it in a wholly original fashion to enhance the mystery and the interpretative possibilities of his work. Here is the poem 'Halaila aravti' (I saw you silent, 1900/1):

> I saw you silent, desolate, tonight
> as I lurked outside your room
> your eyes searching,
> bewildered in the window,
> for your lost soul—

> searching recompense
> for the devotion of your youth,
> and you did not see, my love,
> how I slapped and struggled at your window
> like a terror-stricken dove.

The lines 'searching recompense / for the devotion of your youth' (*bikasht et gemul ḥesed ne'uraikh*) allude to the 'marriage' between God and Israel in the book of Jeremiah:

> Thus says the Lord: 'I remember
> the devotion of your youth [*ḥesed ne'uraikh*],
> your love as a bride,
> how you followed me in the wilderness
> in a land not sown.'   (2:3)

Bialik's use of this allusion suggests that the man and woman in the poem may be husband and wife. However, whereas the husband (God) in Jeremiah *remembers* his bride's (Israel's) devotion and love, in Bialik's poem, chillingly, the woman *searches* (*bikasht*) for the recompense of 'the devotion of your youth'. This implies that the bond between the man and the woman has not been consummated.

At other times, too, a biblical expression replete with associations is applied in a startlingly new context. The following passage from Ezekiel comes from a prophecy against Jerusalem on the verge of its destruction by the Babylonians in 587 BCE:

'And when I passed by you and saw you weltering in your blood [*mitboseset be-damekh*], I said to you in your blood, "Live, and grow up like a plant of the field."' (16: 6–7) In the poem 'Ha-Kayitz gove'a' (Summer is dying, 1905), Bialik adopts the phrase 'weltering in your blood' to depict the fiery autumn leaves and the crimson of the setting sun:

> Summer is dying, stained
>   with gold and purple
> of orchards dropping leaves
> of clouds at twilight
> weltering in their blood.

Again, in 'Yadati be-lel arafel' (I know on a foggy night, 1906), the poet's own role, as he sees himself, is given added dimension through a biblical allusion:

> I know on a foggy night
>   like a star I'll fade
> And no star will know my burial place.

Bialik is quoting from the last paragraph of the Five Books of Moses, describing Moses' death. The substitution of 'no star' for 'no man' might be taken to undercut the authority of the God-in-hiding whose control over the world is no more dependable than predictions through the stars:

> So Moses the servant of the Lord died there in the land of Moab, according to the word of the Lord, and he buried him in the valley in the land of Moab opposite Beth-pe'or; but no man knows the place of his burial. (Deuteronomy 33: 5–6)

The chief source of Bialik's poetic power lay in his uncanny ability to assume the voice of a latter-day prophet while retaining his distinctiveness as a modern poet. Bialik saw the prophets not just as poets but as social reformers and revolutionaries, the conscience of humanity, and as national figures whose fiery message had preserved the Jews in the Diaspora. The earliest of the poems in which Bialik speaks directly as a prophet is 'Akhen hatzir ha'am', which he originally called 'From the

Vision of Isaiah'. As this poem has rhyme and metre, it is unlike prophetic poetry which is generally in free verse. In later neo-biblical poems, such as 'Al ha-Sheḥitah' (On the Slaughter, 1903) and *Be-Ir ha-Haregah* (in which the poet repeatedly addressses the reader as 'Son of Man', a direct allusion to Ezekiel), Bialik employs equally formal rhyme and metre. Only in the poem 'Davar' (The Word, 1904) does Bialik break into free verse (which he was to favour in his neo-prophetic poetry from then on) and the impact is greater than anything he had written previously.

However, in this poetry Bialik diverges from the biblical prophets in offering no message of hope. The poem 'Ve-Haya ki ya'arkhu ha-yamim' (And when the days grow long, 1908), subtitled 'From the visions of the latter-day prophets', is a good example. Though it has topical meaning,[4] it can be read as a satire on the grand biblical prophecies of the coming of the Messiah (Zachariah ch. 9), the resurrection (Ezekiel ch. 37) and the golden age of mankind when 'the wolf will lie down with the lamb' (Isaiah ch. 11). There are no miracles, only boredom, longing and defeated hopes. Cats yawl and scratch; and while men eat their herrings they look for the Messiah in a heap of garbage. Worn-out women with babies at the breast listen for the Messiah:

> Baby lifts head from crib,
> Mouse peeps from hole:
> Isn't the Messiah coming?
> Didn't the bells of his donkey tinkle?
> Maid fanning samovar behind stove
> Sticks coal-black face outside:
> Isn't the Messiah coming?
> Didn't his trumpet sound?

Another illustration of the neo-biblical 'prophecy' devoid of hope is 'Ḥoze lekh beraḥ' (Seer, go flee, 1910), in which Bialik adopts the voice of the prophet Amos. This prophet, who lived in the 8th century BCE, had attacked the king of Israel, Jeroboam II, and predicted his fall. For this reason, Amaziah, the high priest at Bethel, expels him to his home in Judah: 'And Amaziah said to

Amos, "O seer, go, flee away to the land of Judah, and eat bread there, and prophesy there; but never again prophesy at Bethel.'" (7: 12–13). The poet-prophet in 'Ḥoze lekh beraḥ' apparently identifies himself with Amos in that he, too, has encountered rejection by the very people whom he has tried to help. But the poem ends not on a note of hope, like the book of Amos, but with a curse:

> You—you are corrupt and rotten
> Tomorrow you'll be swept away by storm.

Bialik's love poems, too, while frequently alluding to the language and ambience of the Song of Songs, a celebration of normative, ecstatic love, are, as we shall see, full of unsatisfied longing, frustration and despair.

The Talmud and Midrash. The other great pre-modern influence on Bialik was the *aggadah*, the Jewish legends and folklore collected in the Palestinian Talmud (*c.* 400 CE), the Babylonian Talmud (*c.* 500 CE) and in the *midrashim*, the homiletical expositions of Scriptures, which were compiled during the Talmudic period and after. Owing to his years of labour on the *Sefer ha-Aggadah*, Bialik knew the *aggadah* better than any Hebrew poet before or since, and he made masterful use of this mine of literary gems. Some of his most delightful stories are the *aggadot* on King David and King Solomon, retold for children in *Va-Yhi ha-Yom*. In this collection, as in his poems, Bialik often makes changes in the *aggadot*, which are revealing of his own creative personality.[5] At times he used *aggadot* to express things which he could not otherwise say openly. The *aggadah* could circumvent Russian censorship, for it offered a code of sorts by which the poet could communicate deeply personal or national thoughts to his readers.

Bialik's use of *aggadah* has not yet been the subject of a thorough critical study, but some illustrations may be offered here to show the nature of his debt. His central poetic work, *Megillat ha-Esh*, is based largely on the following legend from the Babylonian Talmud, which is set at the time of the defeat of Judah by the Romans in 70 CE:

There is a story of four hundred boys and girls who were taken prisoner to serve as prostitutes. They understood what their fate would be, and they asked, 'If we jump into the sea and drown, will we have a place in the World to Come [suicide being against Jewish law]?' The oldest among them expounded on the verse, 'The Lord said, "I will bring them back from Bashan, I will bring them back from the depths of the sea" [Psalms 68: 22]. 'I will bring them back from Bashan'—from the jaws of lions. 'From the depths of the sea'—those who drown. When the girls heard this, they all leaped into the sea. The boys expounded: if the girls, who would engage in normal sexual relations, can commit this act, we [who would be used in perverse practices] how much more. They too jumped into the sea. Of them it is written in Scripture: 'For thy sake we are slain all day long, and accounted as sheep for the slaughter'. [Psalms 43: 22] (*Gittin* 57b).

Bialik turns this *aggadah* into a powerful, if somewhat fragmented, Romantic allegory of national and personal catastrophe, at the heart of which is the poet's own confession.

The poem 'Mete Midbar' (The Dead of the Wilderness, 1902) also owes its inspiration to a Talmudic *aggadah*, of the Israelites who, as a result of their lack of faith, were prohibited from entering the Land of Israel (Numbers 14: 26 ff.). An Arab merchant is in conversation with a rabbi, Rabba bar Bar Ḥana:

'Come and I will show you the Dead of the Wilderness.' I went with him and saw the dead men looking as though they were ecstatic. They lay supine and the knee of one was lifted. The Arab merchant passed under the knee riding on a camel and holding a spear erect—and he did not touch it. (*Bava Batra* 73b–74a)

In 'Mete Midbar', Bialik converts a tall story into a magisterial allegory of the somnolent condition of the Jews of his time and of their immense latent power, if only they chose to use it.

Another striking illustration of Bialik's use of *aggadah*

appears in his poem 'Akhen gam zeh musar Elohim' (This too is the sweeping scourge, 1904). This 'poem of wrath' is set against the background of rising assimilation among the young generation of Russian Jews, and their rejection of both traditional Judaism and Jewish nationalism. On one level, therefore, Bialik is addressing the Russian Jews directly:

> You'll raise Pithom and Rameses for your oppressors,
> Using your children as bricks;
> When their cry lifts from the wood and the stone—
> It will die before reaching your ears.

Pithom and Rameses (Exodus 1: 11) were cities built by the enslaved Israelites in Egypt. The use of children as bricks appears in a number of Midrashic interpretations,[6] such as the one of Exodus 2: 24: '"And God heard their groaning": Rabbi Akiba said: "Pharaoh's butchers would use the Israelites as mortar in the walls—and the Holy One, Blessed be He, would hear their cries."' In another *aggadah*, the angels in heaven attempt to persuade God not to drown the Egyptians in the sea. The angel Gabriel fetches a brick with a baby sunken into it and declares to God that this was the way the Egyptians treated the Israelites. God then decides against the Egyptians. Bialik recasts these *aggadot* to convey his bitterness and anger that the Jews were wasting their energies in building the cultures of other nations who hated them while ignoring their own heritage.

Paradoxically, when Bialik's message remains ambiguous, his use of *aggadah* reaches its most sophisticated and brilliant expression. The enigmatic lines in the poem 'Ve-Haya ki timtze'u' (And if you find, 1911),

> What he didn't want was given him
> And the one thing he asked-
> he didn't find

refers, among other things, to an *aggadah* based on a rabbinic belief that the serpent in the Garden was sexually drawn to Eve: 'Our rabbis taught: the primeval serpent desired what was not rightfully his. What he sought he did not get; and what he had [a place in Eden] was taken from him' (*Sotah* 9b). This source does not explicate the poem by any means, but it greatly enhances its suggestiveness.

The same is true of Bialik's use of *aggadah* in the poem 'Hetzitz va-Met', which is based on the following: 'Four [rabbis] entered Paradise [or: the realm of mysticism]: Ben Azai and Ben Zoma, Aḥer and Rabbi Akiba... Ben Azai looked and died [*hetzitz va-met*]' (*Ḥagigah* 14b). In Bialik's hands, this *aggadah*, a parable of the dangers of mystical contemplation, is shaped into a brilliant Kafkaesque allegory of man's helplessness and the futility of his endeavours in an indifferent universe:

> And the torch was fading, fading, and the paths
> were getting crooked, and worse—
> One corridor, then another—where was the last
> gate, where was the palace?
>
> ... Then the torch went out, and the gates opened—
> He looked in,
> and his body fell, a smoking brand on its side,
> on the threshold of the void.

Medieval influences. Bialik's influence by medieval Hebrew poetry is not easy to gauge, as much of this poetry was itself influenced by the Bible, and it may also have come to Bialik through its impact on *Haskalah* poetry. Perhaps the deepest impression was made by Judah Halevi's poems of Zion. A number of Bialik's early poems, notably 'El ha-Tzippor', pay indirect homage to Halevi. In combining the deeply personal and the national in his poetry, Bialik was undoubtedly influenced both by Halevi and by the other great medieval Hebrew poet, Solomon ibn Gabirol. 'Shaḥa nafshi' (My spirit is bowed, 1923), takes its title from a devotional lyric by Gabirol, and was written at a time when Bialik and Ravnitzky were editing Gabirol's poems and those of Moses ibn Ezra. Bialik built on the achievements of the medieval Hebrew poets, who were profoundly influenced by Arabic poetry. One of his most successful experiments in verse was the comic farce *Aluf Batzlut ve-Aluf Shum* (Knight of Onions and Knight of Garlic, 1923, 1927), inspired by the *maquama*, a medieval Arabic form in which a story is told in rhyme.

The Haskalah. Bialik seriously began to read *Haskalah* literature as a boy. The allure of this forbidden literature was great to an orphan brought up by a puritanical grandfather. Before he was twenty he was thoroughly well read in the novels of Abraham Mapu, the essays of Peretz Smolenskin, M. L. Lilienblum's autobiography, the poetry of J. L. Gordon and others. Mapu and Smolenskin, in their different ways, stirred his feelings for the Land of Israel. Lilienblum was the first to articulate the crisis of faith with which Bialik himself was to grapple in his poetry. Gordon set the standard for contemporary Hebrew poetry, although he was something of an anachronism even in his own day, for with the gradual emancipation and assimilation of the Jews, Hebrew appeared at times to have little future. (The historian Leopold Zunz is reported to have met him once: on being told that he was a Hebrew poet, Zunz asked facetiously, or in bewilderment, 'When did you live?'[7])

Bialik greatly admired Gordon, though perhaps more as a literary pioneer and as a fighter than as a poet. Gordon, more than any other *Haskalah* poet, furnished Bialik with poetic models to emulate and to react against. When Gordon began writing, in the last years of the reign of Nicholas I, Hebrew poetry was impoverished in talent and lacking in aesthetic standards: Gordon enriched it immeasurably, by introducing a range of new techniques and subjects. In a historical context, Gordon's achievement was immense: he has been unfairly consigned to oblivion. Without him, Bialik would not have had a foundation upon which to build.

Although he provided Bialik with a clear idea of the possibilities of Hebrew verse, Gordon also inadvertently showed him how not to write, a lesson which was equally valuable, if not more so. For Gordon's poems are clever, even ingenious, but rarely moving. They rouse admiration rather than empathy. The style is wooden and it lacks the plastic power to convey the character of the poet. It is overloaded with biblical allusions and full of rhetoric and propaganda, 'a little honey and a lot of sweat',[8] as Bialik put it.

For all Gordon's faults, at the time of his death in 1892 there was no one to replace him. At this time, Bialik wrote a eulogy for him, 'El ha-Aryeh ha-Met' (To the Dead Lion). This poem was meant to be a tribute through imitation, but instead it reads like a parody, in *ottava rima*, no less. With this poem, Bialik effectively laid claim to Gordon's crown: here are a few lines from it:

> Is another lion slain upon the high places?
>
> The poet fell, he fell because he rose to the moon.
>
> You were a jackal to weep our affliction.

Bialik did not include it in his *Collected Poems*.

European and Russian influences. From his late teens onwards, Bialik read widely in European and Russian literature, mostly in German and Russian.[9] (He first learned to read Russian in Volozhin in 1890–1 and German in Odessa in 1891–2.) The chief foreign influences on Bialik were the Romantic poets of the late eighteenth and early nineteenth century, such as Lermontov, Lessing and Schiller, together with Pushkin and Goethe. He knew Byron's *Hebrew Melodies* and Heine's *Hebraische Melodien*, and translated Heine's 'Prinzessin Sabbath' into Yiddish. While still a young man he read at least some of Gogol, Nietzsche, Cervantes and Tolstoy. His folk poems, similarly, were greatly influenced by the Slavic folk poems with which he had grown up. Among the strongest known influences on Bialik in the early part of his career were the Russian poems of Zion of the Russian-Jewish poet Simon Frug. And, of course, he was influenced by contemporary Hebrew writers, such as M. Y. Berdichewsky, Saul Tchernichowsky and M. Z. Feierberg.

Indirectly, too, through the *Haskalah* and later through his fellow writers, most of whom were extremely well read, Bialik became familiar with the main currents of modern

European literature. However, the primary effect of this literature on him was that it set an artistic standard which he attempted to equal in Hebrew.

Of inestimable importance in Bialik's evolution as an artist was the traditional role of literature in Russian life. In his introduction to Turgenev's novel *Fathers and Sons*, Isaiah Berlin points out that as a result of political repression, literature assumed a greater significance in Russia than in most countries. What was true in 1861, when this novel appeared, was generally true until the revolution (and after):

> Acute shame or furious indignation caused by the misery and degradation of a system in which human beings— serfs—were viewed as 'baptized property', together with a sense of impotence before the rule of injustice, stupidity and corruption, tended to drive pent-up imagination and moral feeling into the only channels that the censorship had not completely shut off—literature and the arts. Hence the notorious fact that in Russia social and political thinkers turned into poets and novelists, while creative thinkers often became publicists. Any protest against institutions, no matter what its origin or purpose, under an absolute despotism is *eo ipso* a political act. Consequently literature became the battleground on which the central social and political issues of life were fought out.[10]

The moral authority of art was all that could challenge corrupt political authority. In this respect, Russian and Hebrew literature were not dissimilar: just as Russian literature foreshadowed the revolution, so also Hebrew literature acted as the midwife for the birth of Jewish nationalism.

Bialik had to steer carefully between the Scylla of censorship and the Charybdis of ideological propaganda. Russian censorship under Tsarist rule was far more lax and inefficient than after the revolution. Moreover censors were often corrupt and could be bribed. Nevertheless, the fact that censorship existed meant that Russian writers automatically, perhaps unconsciously, censored themselves, for they generally knew how far they could go. Through the use of classical Jewish sources and by setting his poetry in the past, in a biblical or *aggadic* milieu, Bialik could evade censorship. (In this respect, ironically, censorship actually improved the quality of Bialik's art.) 'En zot, ki rabat tzerartunu' was passed by the censor as it was originally called 'Bar Kochba', thus safely setting it in the 2nd century CE. *Be-Ir ha-Haregah* got past with the title *Masah Nemirov* (The Burden of Nemirov), after a Polish village in which Jews were massacred by the Cossacks in 1648–9.

Another potential danger was the Russian tradition of using literature for educational purposes. Vissarion Belinsky (1811–1848), the foremost Russian critic of the nineteenth century, had insisted that literature must have a message and be used as a tool for social change: Russia was such a backward country that there was no choice. This rejection of art for art's sake influenced the *Maskilim* and, later, Ahad Ha'am. In his manifesto setting forward the aims of *Ha-Shiloah* in 1896, he echoed Belinski in calling on Hebrew writers to abandon free creativity and to harness their energies to the national cause.[11] This view of Hebrew literature was to cause Bialik a good deal of anguish and guilt.

In other respects, Russia exerted a positive influence on Bialik. He is unmistakably a Russian poet, with the energy, the moral sincerity and torment, the chiaroscuro moods, the love of the Russian landscape and the changing seasons, which characterize Russian poetry. Russia is as much the subject of Bialik's poetry as Zion or his inner world. For all his alienation from the land of his birth and his commitment to Zionism, Bialik maintained a deep love for the Ukrainian landscape in which he had grown up. Though he dreamed of the Carmel and the Lebanon, and of Jerusalem's ruins, he was a poet of Radi, of the hills, woods and streams of Volhynia. These made an impression which lasted throughout his life. 'Here before me,' he wrote of Radi in *Safiah*, 'on this backcloth of blue skies and green grass are embroidered the pictures of my world in those first days, wonderful pictures, light and calm as pure mists, half secrets and half dreams—and nevertheless no scenes are bright and clear as they are, nor any reality as real.'[12]

This love for the homeland coupled with deep disappointment

and rage is found in Tchernichowsky's poems (which probably influenced Bialik's in this regard), and in Russian literature generally. Tolstoy, for example, and more recently Solzhenitsyn, have shown similar ambivalence towards their beautiful but cruel land. Here are some lines from 'Mi-Shire ha-Ḥoref' (Winter Songs, 1902), one of Bialik's most exuberant poems, describing the Russian winter:

> No end of the whiteness, of splendour
> From bottom to top, house to tree.
>
> Snow made pure in thirteen sieves
> Coats it all like opaque glass.
>
> Roofs like alabaster hats,
> One side white, the other blue,
>
> Shining out to the sun and all—
> Ravens alone dot them black,
>
> Screeching, sliding over the glaze,
> Pecking, scratching—suddenly gone.

Mendele. Among Hebrew writers at the turn of the century, Bialik had only one model of undisputed artistic excellence—the novelist Mendele Mokher Sefarim (Mendele the Bookseller), pseudonym of S. J. Abramowitz (1836?–1917). Mendele has the unique distinction of being the first great artist and seminal figure in two literatures—Yiddish and modern Hebrew. In the 1870s and 1880s he wrote a number of novels which established him as the leading Yiddish writer of the age and which constitute the fullest and most devastating literary portrait of the Jews in the Pale of Settlement. They are characterized by a potent mixture of cruel satire and caricature and loving humour, expressing Mendele's deep ambivalence towards his people, for they are grimy and downtrodden, yet they preserve traces of their former nobility. After the pogroms Mendele began to rework (not merely to translate) these novels into Hebrew, a task which continued for most of the last twenty years of his life. This enterprise was the most important contribution to Hebrew fiction before Agnon, indeed it marks the beginning of modern Hebrew fiction as art. In the process of writing these novels, Mendele created a brilliant, flexible, highly influential style. 'No Hebrew author,' writes the Israeli critic Gershon Shaked, 'is more original in revealing the treasures of the Hebrew language.'[13] In particular, Mendele made masterful use of Talmudic sources. At the same time, he was greatly influenced by European literature, by Cervantes, Gogol, Dickens and others, although he did not use these sources as well as the Jewish ones. Mendele's successful harmonization of traditional Jewish literature and European models exerted a powerful influence upon his younger contemporaries.

Bialik was in close contact with Mendele from the time of his arrival in Odessa in 1900 until the older man's death shortly after the October 1917 revolution. He regarded himself as Mendele's disciple and had unstinting admiration for his achievement (though he also believed that Mendele's style was virtually incomprehensible to anyone who had not received a traditional Jewish education). Jacob Fichman, a friend and colleague of Bialik, wrote that Bialik regarded Mendele 'not as a human being but as one of the wonders of nature'.[14] He frequently paid homage to Mendele as the creator of modern Hebrew prose style, and he published the first edition of Mendele's *Collected Works* in Hebrew (1909–12). For a short time after his arrival in Odessa he worked with Mendele on the translation into Hebrew of Mendele's Yiddish classic, *Fishke der Krummer* (Fishke the Lame). His own prose fiction—'Aryeh Ba'al Guf', 'Me-Aḥore ha-Gader' and *Safiaḥ*—is, on his own admission, deeply indebted to Mendele.

We may mention just one of the many ways in which Mendele influenced Bialik. Before Mendele, childhood had hardly figured in Hebrew literature: in his works it is a central theme. For most of the time that Bialik knew him, Mendele was writing the two biographical works in which childhood loss is prominent: *Be-Emek ha-Bakha* (In the Valley of Tears, 1896–1908) and *Ba-Yamim ha-Hem* (In Those Days, 1903–17). In his writings, Mendele is more a social historian than a psychologist of childhood, depicting the lost childhood of his characters virtually as a symbol of the life of the Russian Jews. Yet in a number of ways he paved the way for Bialik's accounts of childhood: in his recognition of children as human beings in their own right and his ability to enter their world; in his emphasis on the importance of childhood loss and mourning; the description of conditions for mourning and the sense of utter abandonment after the loss; the idea of a childhood paradise lost; the turn inward after loss to a world of private fantasy, particularly to the world of *aggadah*.[15] All this, as we shall see, is of great importance in understanding Bialik's finest prose work, *Safiah*, as well as many of his poems.

It may be that Bialik was drawn to Mendele partly because their childhood experiences had been similar. He, too, though at a somewhat earlier age than Mendele, had lost his father and been separated from his mother. Like Mendele, too, he had little support in his grief and his conditions for mourning were poor. His deep, almost filial affection for Mendele—he always called him *Saba*, 'grandfather'—an affection which was reciprocated, was owing in no small measure to these shared traumas.

Ahad Ha'am. As Mendele was Bialik's artistic mentor, Ahad Ha'am provided him with ideological direction. He seems also to have helped to fill the void left by the death of the poet's father. Bialik looked upon Ahad Ha'am with reverence and awe, and he described him as the decisive influence in his life.[16] After his death in 1927, Bialik eulogized him, saying that the entire generation was orphaned by this loss.

Ahad Ha'am was the creator of the modern Hebrew essay, which he raised to a European standard. Bialik began reading him before he came to Volozhin, in 1889 when he was sixteen. He was drawn to Ahad Ha'am, he recalled, not just for the ideas and the style but mainly for the personality behind the ideas, steeped in European literature and philosophy, thoroughly immersed in Jewish literature and history, and driven by a powerful spiritual sense of purpose. Ahad Ha'am's aim was to transform traditional religious Judaism into a national force. Zionism, he insisted, was not merely a secular political response to anti-Semitism, it was latent in the Jewish religion and a natural expression of Jewish religious consciousness. The Jewish national reawakening, accordingly, would have to involve a spiritual and cultural revival in the Land of Israel, and nowhere else. Zionism, he argued, was pointless if detached from the traditional values of Judaism, from the Hebrew language and literature, from the age-old bond between the Jewish people and the Land of Israel. The redemption of the Jewish people was hindered by weakness of will, but this could be overcome. These ideas were expressed in a crisp, direct Hebrew style, suggesting to Bialik more the character of a businessman (which Ahad Ha'am was) than a typical literary man. In his view, Ahad Ha'am was a great healer. At a time when the Russian Jews had suffered a terrible blow, psychological as well as physical and material, he helped them on the road to recovery. He helped to restore their self-confidence and self-esteem, offering through nationalism a solution to the crisis of faith which beset his generation.

Dov Sadan and others have suggested that the growth of Bialik's poetic gift was stunted by Ahad Ha'am's influence.[17] To him, Bialik's gift was valuable mainly insofar as it could be enlisted in the national cause: he had little, if any, regard for art for art's sake. As the great philosopher of cultural Zionism, a key member of the *Hibbat Zion* in Odessa and founder and editor of *Ha-Shiloah*, he had a pre-eminent place in Hebrew letters at the turn of the century. Bialik himself wrote repeatedly of the overwhelming effect which Ahad Ha'am's writings had upon him, though he hardly knew him personally in Odessa. His reverence for him as a unique spiritual leader is apparent also in the poems 'Le-Ahad Ha'am' (To Ahad Ha'am, 1903) and 'Al-kef yam-mavet zeh' (On this dead-sea cliff, 1906).

This influence waned after Ahad Ha'am left *Ha-Shiloah* in 1903 (he was succeeded by Joseph Klausner and Bialik); and after he left Odessa for London in 1906, as Bialik wrote, 'the *Shekhinah* [divine presence] had abandoned him.'[18] 'Al-kef yam-mavet zeh' expresses Bialik's desolation at this loss. Bialik was only thirty when Ahad Ha'am left *Ha-Shiloah* and had only just found his voice as a poet. In his most productive years, 1903–11, he had virtually a free hand to write and to publish everything that he wrote, and when he stopped writing poetry in 1911, he did so mainly for private, not ideological, reasons. However, there is little reason to believe that even in the 1890s, when Ahad Ha'am's influence was at its strongest, Bialik was adversely affected by him. It is true that Ahad Ha'am conceived of Bialik as the great national poet, who would embody in his art his own ideology. Bialik's sense of guilt at being preoccupied with personal rather than national matters was undoubtedly exacerbated by his attachment to Ahad Ha'am. But this did not stop him from writing confessional lyrics—it may even have given his poetry an edge which it would not have had otherwise. A large number of his pre-1903 poems have little, if any, national content. When he wrote about national themes he did so out of conviction, not to gain Ahad Ha'am's approval. Poems that Ahad Ha'am turned down for *Ha-Shiloah*—he rejected 15 out of a total of 31—Bialik sent elsewhere or published at a later date.

Far from suppressing Bialik's poetic gift, Ahad Ha'am enabled it to develop. He gave Bialik much encouragement and artistic direction when he most needed it, during his literary apprenticeship in the 1890s. He set far higher standards than had existed previously in modern Hebrew (Bialik's own essays owe much to him) and established a new and firm ideological basis for Hebrew literature. In doing so, he conferred upon Hebrew writers a status which they had not had previously and increased their motivation to create. To the end of his life, Bialik loved and admired Ahad Ha'am, but in his art he eventually went his own way.

4

ROMANTIC-NATIONAL POET

Bialik's career as a poet may be divided into three main phases: the years of apprenticeship in the 1890s; the Odessa years, 1900–11, followed by the *shtika* which was interrupted by a brief period of creativity in 1915; and the final years, 1922–34, when most of his relatively small output was written during his travels in Europe.

From the start, even in his juvenilia, Bialik's poetry was astonishingly mature, confident and technically accomplished. Most of his central themes, techniques, and the main outline of the poet's self-presentation appear in the early poems. Though not among Bialik's best—in translation some of them are apt to sound banal—they are fascinating for what they reveal of Bialik's growth as a poet, and they repay close study in the original. One major theme of the 1890s, however, is not built on in the post-1900 period. Quintessential Zionist poems such as 'Birkhat Am' (Blessing of the People, 1894) or 'La-Mitnadvim ba-Am' (To the Volunteers, 1899), offering faith, hope and courage to the pioneers in the Land of Israel and to the Jews in the Diaspora are not continued after 1900.

    The poems of the 1890s embody a paradox which holds true throughout Bialik's career: although the poetry overflows with emotion, it is at the same time carefully thought out and tightly controlled. Bialik shows much technical virtuosity in mastering strong emotion and giving it form. The importance which he attached to the discipline of rhyme and metre may be seen in the fact that until 1897 he did not produce a single poem in free verse.[1] There is something in Bialik which T. S. Eliot found in the English Metaphysical poets: a striking combination of intellect and feeling.

Practically each one of Bialik's poems is shaped differently and distinctively. In many of his early poems he favours the four-line stanza rhyming ABCB, with the rhyming lines generally shorter than the non-rhyming ones, giving dramatic punch to the poems. This form is used superbly in a number of the post-1900 poems, such as 'Hetzitz va-Met'.

The self-confessional streak which came to dominate his poetry in the years leading up to the *shtika*, is also strongly evident in the 1890s. We learn a good deal about the poet: for example, he has been abandoned as a child ('Be-Yom stav' [An Autumn Day, 1897?]); he feels, partly in consequence, that he is inwardly wounded ('Shirat Yisrael' [Poem of Israel, 1894]); he has suffered great poverty at least at one point in his early life ('Mi-Shut ba-merhakim' [After long wanderings, 1891]); his relationships with women arouse much inner conflict ('Eyneha' [Her Eyes, 1892]); he is or was an orthodox Jew and remains deeply attached to Jewish tradition ('Al Saf Bet ha-Midrash'); he has a rather low view of himself, is troubled by feelings of guilt and inadequacy, and predicts a sorry end for himself ('Dimah Ne'emanah' [Faithful Tear, 1895]); he attaches more hope to his people than to himself ('La-Mitnadvim ba-Am'); he frequently uses imagery of unfruitfulness and rottenness to depict himself ('El ha-Tzippor'). Yet, in flashes he shows much *joie de vivre* and a great love for the world around him. This picture of the poet is consistent with that in the later poems and with what is known of the man himself.

Despite their occasional sentimentality and imitation of European Romantic poetry, these poems have retained much of their appeal. One senses in them a powerful, almost hypnotic compulsion to explore and lay bare complex inner states. One of the key poems of this period is 'Raze Laila' (Night Secrets, 1898–9). This poem touches a new chord in Hebrew, suggesting a depth of personality which had rarely been plumbed before in secular Hebrew poetry. Although, again, not one of Bialik's finest poems, 'Raze Laila' looks forward to the great poems of Bialik's maturity, such as 'Lifne Aron ha Sefarim' (Before the Bookcase, 1910):

As if my eyes were gouged out, as if
I were beheaded
with a sharp, heavy axe—so thickly
bandaged round me the darkness
covering everything, the synagogue too . . .
This, the bent giant, shadowing
the houses beneath him.

Another key poem of the 1890s is 'Be-Yom stav', with which Bialik opened the first two collections of his poetry (1901, 1908). Here for the first time he attempts to convey the impact of his separation from his mother when he was seven. The mother is described virtually as his poetic muse driving him to create. Her memory is inseparably bound up with the pain of separation.[2]

Within a short time after Bialik arrived in Odessa in 1900 his poetry underwent a momentous change. Other twentieth-century poets, including W. B. Yeats and T. S, Eliot, went through a similar transformation, but not so rapidly. Almost overnight Bialik's poems became shorter and leaner, conveying an almost Blakean compression and energy. The poem 'Lo zakhiti ba-or min ha-hefker' (I did not gain the light from nothing, 1902) is one of the most interesting poems of this period. The poet, with new-found confidence, proclaims the uniqueness of his gift:

One spark hides in my flinty heart,
Just one spark—but it's all mine,
Neither borrowed nor stolen—
but from me, within me.

The cause or causes of Bialik's artistic metamorphosis in 1900–1 will probably never be known for certain. The poems in question deal with the same themes of the 1890s, but with greater intensity and a sense of crisis. The changed circumstances in which he was writing must have affected his style. Bialik was born and brought up in a largely rural community—to the end of his life he regarded himself as a country boy at heart—and after his first visit to Odessa in 1891–2 he had returned to small-town life in Korosten and Sosnowiec. He was virtually isolated from his fellow writers, communicating with them by post. Now, in the sprawling Black Sea port, he found himself in an exciting and challenging new environment. Odessa was the most Western, cosmopolitan city in the Pale of Settlement, with an unusually large Jewish population of about 140,000.[3] Here Bialik quickly became part of a remarkable community of writers, including Ahad Ha'am, Mendele, Ravnitzky and Simon Dubnow, as well as a group of promising younger writers such as Zalman Schneour, Jacob Fichman and S. Ben Zion, who soon came to regard Bialik as their literary master. Odessa was a relatively prosperous and liberal city. The Jews there were bowed down neither by overwhelming poverty nor by anti-Semitism and rabbinic strictures, as in other parts of the Pale. As a port-city, Odessa had a refreshingly earthy, free-wheeling tang. (It is interesting that the best-known literary creation living in pre-1914 Odessa was Isaac Babel's Benya Krik, the Jewish gangster.) From Odessa one could see more clearly beyond Russia. Here the Russian Zionist movement was born and was flourishing, and Hebrew literature was respected and encouraged. There could be no better place for a Hebrew poet at the time.

There is a certain irony in the fact that Bialik's return to the home of Ahad Ha'am marked the end of his 'Zionist' phase. Judging from his early poems in Odessa, 1900–3, Bialik was concerned mainly with the perfection of his art, testing himself against the great nineteenth-century Romantics.[4] In 1901 he published the first of his folk-poems, 'Mi yode'a ir Lishtina?' (Who knows the town of Lishtin?). From this time, his lyrics show increasing aural delicacy; many of them are easily set to music, and they remind the reader that the Hebrew for poetry, *shirah*, means 'song'. Here is one of the lyrics of this period, 'Yam ha-demamah polet sodot':

> The sea of quiet spits secrets,
> The world is still:
> The river-sound is ceaseless
> Behind the mill.

Darkness conquers all,
Piling shadows on:
Stars in the dark fall
One by one.

When the world falls silent,
I feel my heart beating;
The slow flow of the fount
Leaping.

To myself I say, 'My son,
Your dreams come true;
Believe me, stars have fallen,
Not for you.

Your star is fixed
Shining in its orbit;
Look! it sends you hints
Of comfort.'

When the world falls silent
I'll watch my star;
One world alone is mine—
The one in my heart.

The Poems of Wrath

For about three years, from the time of his arrival in Odessa until the outbreak of the pogrom in Kishinev in April 1903, Bialik worked almost entirely as a private lyric poet, with hardly an echo of national sentiment in his work. By now he was recognized as the finest living Hebrew poet, but he was still a minor poet by European standards. The American poet Randall Jarrell once defined a minor poet as one who spends a lifetime standing out in thunderstorms and is struck by lightning half a dozen times; a great poet is struck a dozen or more times. The pogroms acted on Bialik like a powerful electrical storm galvanizing him into becoming a major Romantic-national poet. (In some of his poems he actually uses imagery of explosive natural forces, such as earthquakes or storms, to depict himself, his wrath over the atrocities around him.) The still, small voice of the aesthete with one world alone, 'The one in my heart', using precise metre and rhyme, was transformed into the wild, powerful voice of the prophet speaking on behalf of his people and of outraged humanity at large. Most of the 'Poems of Wrath' of the 1903–6 period were written in free verse, as if his former techniques could not fully express and contain his passion. The pogroms seem also to have driven Bialik more deeply into himself, forcing him to confront more directly than previously a host of obsessions, private as well as national. The turning point was reached with the poem 'Al ha-Shehitah' (On the Slaughter), written the month after the Kishinev pogrom, shortly before Bialik paid his fateful visit there. What might have disturbed him most was that children had been murdered. As a childless man who adored children, he was profoundly shocked:

> Heaven, beg mercy for me!
> If you have a God, and he can be reached
> —but I've not found him—
> pray for me!
> My heart is numb, my prayer gone,
> I've lost my strength and hope—
> How long, till when, how long?
>
> Hangman! here's my neck—
> Yours the power, the axe. Let me die
> a dog's death, the world my scaffold—
> We—we the few!
> My blood is cheap—smash skull,
> Let babies' blood and of old men stain you
> forever, for all time.
>
> If there is justice—let it come now!
> But if it comes after I'm destroyed—
> let its throne be wrecked forever!
> let the heavens rot in eternal evil;
> Go, wicked men, in violence,
> Live on your blood, wash in it.

Cursed be he who cries: Avenge!
Such vengeance, of a child's blood
Satan has not yet devised—
let the blood seep to the depth!
eat at the darkness, dig up
the rotten foundations
of the earth.

After a stay of several weeks in Kishinev, Bialik retreated in July 1903 to his in-laws' home in the forest of Gorovshchin where he wrote *Be-Ir ha-Haregah*. The poem shows how deeply the visit to Kishinev had stirred him and altered his perspective. In 'Al ha-Sheḥitah' he had accused the perpetrators, including, indirectly, the Russian government; *Be-Ir ha-Haregah* is a massive indictment of the Jews.[5] Moving like a funeral procession, the poem tells, at times with nauseating detail, of a journey into hell, revisiting the scenes of violence, the streets and yards stained with blood, the vandalized houses, the cellars where women were raped and their children murdered. The explosion of sarcasm and bitterness to which this leads at the end of the poem has for its target the cowardly, parasitical survivors who roused Bialik's ire for using this national tragedy to elicit sympathy and funds for themselves:

Away, you beggars, to the charnel-house
The bones of your father disinter!
Cram them into your knapsacks, bear
Them on your shoulders, and go forth
To do your business with these precious wares
At all the country fairs . . .[6]

With *Be-Ir ha-Haregah*, Bialik began the most intense creative period of his life. His poems of this period move in two seemingly contrary directions. There are the quiet, inturned lyrics, which continue the path he had begun before 1903, but there are also the fierce, public, intensely angry poems which express the tumult of the external world as well as internal tumult. The main catalyst for these latter poems was the wave of pogroms which continued intermittently until 1906, but they also reflect such matters as the discord within the Zionist movement; the Russo-Japanese war (1904–5); the death of Herzl on 4 July 1904; the 1905 revolution and the *Potemkin* mutiny; the Tsar's reluctant concession of civil rights in October 1905 and the violence which followed. The 'Poems of Wrath' gave expression to the sense of outrage and powerlessness felt by the Russian Jews and also the aggressiveness which led to increased militancy, especially among the young, and the formation for the first time of Jewish defence groups. (As pointed out previously, in the years 1903–4 about half of those sentenced for political offences in Russia were Jews.) In this respect, the 'Poems of Wrath' mark a major turning point in modern Jewish history, the beginning of a profound change in the Jewish consciousness and the emergence from powerlessness.

'Davar' (The Word), written several weeks after Herzl's death, conveys the despair of the Jewish people at the loss of their charismatic leader. (This loss might also have revived Bialik's memories of his father's death.) This was also a period of bitter wrangling within the Zionist movement, particularly over Herzl's plan to accept a British protectorate for the Jewish people in East Africa, which was eventually defeated in 1905. One of the curious features of this poem is that only mid-way ('Dig a grave for us'—in the Hebrew, the exact middle) does it emerge that the poet-prophet is being addressed not by God but by his own people. The psychological premise of this poem is clearer in the light of other poems. At its heart is the poet's ambivalence towards his own role. He imagines the wrath of his people at him for his inadequacy and at those who (like the poet himself?) use national or communal objects—the coal, spark or altar—for purely personal ends. This accusation recalls that in *Be-Ir ha-Haregah*, as well as *Megillat ha-Esh*. In the latter part of the poem, Bialik appears to convey not only the desperation which drove hundreds of thousands of Russian Jews to emigrate during the years 1904–14 but also the burden of Jewish suffering throughout history. The rough pattern of 'Davar', the first 'poem of wrath' written in free verse, is of alternating long and short lines, occasionally reminiscent in rhythm and sound of the biblical *kinah* (lament):

Hurl, O prophet, from your altar the fiery coal,
Leave it to the churls—
Theirs to roast meat, to heat the pot
To warm their hands,
Scatter, prophet, from your flinty heart
The spark—
To light their cigarettes
To light up the sneer on their faces, lurking
Thief-like, and the malice in their eyes.
Here they come, the churls
The prayer you taught them on their lips,
They feel your pain, they hope your hope—they cry
For your ruined altar;
Later they'll swoop to the ruin, poke about
Pull out the cracked stones
To fit in their house floors, their garden walls
And use for tombstones;
When they find your heart, charred in the rubble—
They'll throw it to their dogs.

Kick in shame at your altar, turn your back
On its fire and smoke.
Wipe off the spider webs from the harp
Of your heart strings
Woven into a song of revival,
     a vision of salvation—
A false prophecy—
Scatter them to the wind,
To wander, tattered, pale, in the world's emptiness
On a clear day at summer's end
So that no silver string or web will see another again,
But perish on the first rainy day;
Your hammer, your iron hammer, broken
   from too much use
On hearts of stone,
Break and break again and pound into a shovel,
Dig a grave for us.
Whoever puts the word of God in your mouth—

Damn him fearlessly.
Even if your word is bitter as death, or death itself—
Let us hear it and know.
Look, how night envelops us, we are crushed
By darkness, we grope like the blind;
Something has gone wrong, no one knows what,
No one sees, no one tells,
If the sun has risen for us or set—
Or set forever.
And chaos is all around, all around terrible chaos
and no escape;
As our voices entreating lift into the darkness—
Whose ear will turn?
As our raw blasphemy streams to heaven—
Over whose crown will it trickle?
Grinding tooth, knuckling ire-veined fists—
On whose scalp will the fury drift?
All will fall   windily
Down the throat of chaos;
No comfort remains, no helping hand, no way out—
And heaven is dumb;
Murdering us with dispassionate eyes,
Bearing its blame in blood-torn silence.
Open your mouth, prophet of doom,
If you have anything to say—speak!
If it's bitter as death, or death itself,
Speak!
Why should we fear death—
      his angel rides on our shoulder,
His bridle in our mouths;
With a cry of revival and the whoops of players
We'll stagger into the grave.

Bialik followed 'Davar' with 'Akhen gam zeh musar Elohim'
in the autumn of 1904.[7] This is an anguished condemnation of
Jewish assimilationists, particularly those in Russia, who gained
strength during the troubles of 1903–6, and who saw the socialist
and revolutionary movements as a viable alternative both to

Tsarist rule and to traditional Judaism which they felt had failed
them. Yet the force of this poem, like that of the other 'Poems of
Wrath', seems to well up largely from unconscious personal
obsessions. Childlessness or the loss of children, as in 'Al
ha-Shehitah', always evoked pity and outrage in Bialik. The
closing lines of the poem, like those of 'Davar', recall Bialik's
accounts of his family's dire poverty and despair after his father's
death.[8]

This too is the sweeping scourge
　　of the Lord's chastisement—
Though you deny it to your heart;
So you'll scatter your sacred tear　across all oceans
And string it on to each false ray of light;
And pour your spirit into all the marble of foreign lands
And sink your life into the bosom of strange stone;
And as your flesh drips blood between the teeth
　　of your destroyers—
You'll let them have your soul.
You'll raise Pithom and Rameses for your oppressors,
Using your children as bricks;
When their cry lifts from the wood and the stone—
It will die before reaching your ears.
If an eagle rises among your sons and grows wings—
You'll send him away forever;
When he soars, sun-thirsty, powerful, above—
Not to you will he bring down the luminaries;
When he splits through the clouds with his pinions
Paving a path for the beam of light—
Not to you will it fall;
Far away, on some craggy peak, he'll cry out
But the echo won't reach you.
One by one, will you lose your dear ones
And be childless.
Your home will be stripped of its splendour,
Your tent put to ruin.
Sickening desolation will creep in,
Threshold untouched by God's grace,

Window unshaken by the joyful knock of salvation.
Your prayer will stifle in the cracks,
You'll search fruitlessly for tears of compassion:
The heart will choke, like a cluster of squeezed grapes
Thrust into the corner of the vat,
Yielding not a drop to revive the soul
That overflows with longing.
You will grope in the furnace of the ruin—
And find its stones cold,
A shrieking cat in the chill of its ash.
You will sit solitary, mourning,
Torrents in the world, dust and ashes in the heart,
And you'll stare at the dead flies on the windows
And the spiders in empty corners,
And poverty will wail at you in the chimney,
The walls of the ruin will tremble with cold—

Bialik spent 1904 as an editor of *Ha-Shiloah* in Warsaw, where he wrote 'Davar' and 'Akhen gam zeh musar Elohim'. At the time of his return to Odessa in January 1905, Russia entered its deepest crisis before the revolution. That month 200,000 workers protesting against the government were fired on by Tsarist troops who killed several hundred and wounded over a thousand. The next month the Russian government created the anti-Semitic organization the Black Hundreds, with the aim of diverting general dissatisfaction with the government and revolutionary unrest on to the Jews. Pogroms broke out in Feodosiya in February, in Melitopol in April, in Zhitomir in May. The crisis worsened when in May two-thirds of the Russian Imperial fleet was destroyed by the Japanese off the south coast of Korea. Over 100,000 men were lost in the war with the Japanese. In June the *Potemkin* mutiny broke out. Later that summer, the anti-Semitic forgery *The Protocols of the Elders of Zion* was published. In October general strikes broke out across Russia. The Tsar capitulated by granting a constitutional government with a legislature (Duma). Immediately, pogroms broke out in hundreds of towns and villages in southern Russia: the worst was in Odessa. On 8 November Bialik wrote to his friend Ben-Ami:

Everything written in the newspapers outside the Pale about what is going on here is nothing compared to the reality. Today they finish burying the dead—over 300 Jews killed. Over 600 of the hooligans were killed. Much wanton destruction. About twenty thousand homeless. The Moldovanka [an Odessa slum area where most of the Jewish poor lived] has been completely decimated. The army and the police joined the hooligans in the riots and murder. If not for our courageous defenders, we'd all have been murdered.[9]

(By this time, about thirty Jewish defence groups were active in Russia.)

The poem 'Yadati be-lel arafel', the last of the 'Poems of Wrath', was written in the wake of the pogroms. In one unbroken sentence (from 'Oh, if only your grief'), the poet prophesies that the murder of his people would become a stigma on the conscience of the world. He foresees violence to the end of time:

> I know on a foggy night
>   like a star I'll fade
> And no star will know my burial place,
> But my fury will smoke after me like a volcano
> After the eruption,
> To be with you while the Wheel still thunders round
> And the ocean rages.
> Oh, if only your grief too were kept alive
> In the world's wide heart,
> Infusing it with life
> So that the sky and the earth, the stars and grass
> Would drink its pain,
> Grow old and be renewed in it, die and flower again,
> Without name, shape, homeland
> A witness of your torture to the last generation,
> Silently crying out to hell and heaven
> Stopping the world's redemption;
> For when at the end of time
>   the sun will shine its righteous deceit
>   over the heads of your slain,

And the banner of hypocrisy
   stained with your blood, mocking heaven, will wave
Over the heads of your murderers,
And God's forged seal, engraved on the banner,
   will pierce the eyes of the sun,
And the dance of arrogant foot,
   the trumpet of the feast of deceit, will shake
Your holy bones in the grave—
And the sky's radiance will tremble,
      darken in your grief,
And the sun will be a stain of your innocent blood,
A mark of Cain on the world's forehead,
A sign that the broken arm of God
Failed,
Star to star will whisper: See the horrible lie!
Look at the awful grief!
Then the God of Vengeance, with injured heart
     will rise and roar—
And storm out with his sword.

At the same time as the 'Poems of Wrath', Bialik continued to write poems of love and nature poems which are as tender and quiet as the others are rough and loud. Yet these two styles appear to complement each other, to make one whole. As in the poetry of Shakespeare, in which similar extremes are found, of tenderness, sexual disgust and wrath, Bialik's poetry seems to repeat the same themes over and over again in different variations. The poet Ted Hughes, writing of Shakespeare, has argued that 'the poetry has its taproot in a sexual dilemma of a particularly black and ugly sort'.[10] The same might be said of Bialik's poetry of Eros, much of it neither love poetry nor erotic poetry but poetry about the lack or failure of love. In 'Ha-Eynayim ha-re'evot' (Hungry Eyes, 1897?), for example, sexual pleasure ends in utter failure and disgust:[11]

These hungry eyes, these lips
    thirsting to be kissed,
These breasts languishing to be touched,
All your hidden precious parts
Sated as even Sheol could not guess;
Your majestic body, the fullness of desire,
All the flesh that gorged me,
The blessing of the well of joy—

If you only knew, beautiful woman,
How I despised it when sated.

I was innocent, no storm of lust
    had fouled me
Till you came. I, foolish boy,
cast down at your feet, mercilessly,
my purity of heart and soul,
the tender flowers of my youth.

For a moment I was infinitely happy,
I blessed the hand that stroked
    its sweet pain;
in this moment, the whole world
        collapsed on me—
how great the price I paid for your flesh!

In another poem, 'Manginah le-Ahavah' (A Song to Love), written during Bialik's engagement in early 1893 and originally dedicated to his fiancée,[12] the poet lays bare his fears of marriage. He plays disturbingly on biblical imagery of sexual incapacity, alluding to the law in the book of Deuteronomy that 'He whose testicles are crushed [petzua daka] or whose male member is cut off shall not enter into the assembly of the Lord' (23 : 2):

What use is the life you've breathed in me
    if it's wounded to despair [im petzuah ad daka] . . .

'Mikhtav katan li katva' (She wrote me a short letter, 1896–7) explores further the motif of a flawed sexual attachment. In this poem the poet is inclined to a Platonic bond with his beloved. Bialik once said that the idea for this poem came to him during

his engagement, when he was on his way to see his future wife.[13]
The poet's beloved sends him an enigmatic letter full of anguish.
He replies:

> You're too saintly
>   to sit by me.
> Be my God and angel,
> I'll pray to you
>   and worship you.

Later poems, such as 'Halaila aravti' and 'Im dimdume
ha-ḥamah' (At twilight, 1902), are bitter portraits of couples
who live in a torment of frustration, longing and isolation. Here
is 'Im dimdume ha-ḥamah':

> At twilight come to the window,
>   lean against me
> Envelop my neck with your arms,
>   press your head against mine—
> Cleave to me.

> And we'll cleave with silent desire,
>   we will look up
> to the awful radiance, let fly our fantasies
>   like doves
> Across the seas of light

> Till they vanish silently on the horizon,
>   in yearning flight,
> Come to rest on purple ridges
>   of cloud
> Islands of splendour.

> Distant islands, lofty worlds
>   of our dreams
> They made us into strangers
>   wherever we went
> They made our lives hell.

Golden islands we thirsted for
    as for a homeland
All the stars hinted
    at them
With trembling light.

And on these islands we remain,
    friendless, like two flowers
in a desert, two lost souls searching
    for an eternal loss
In a foreign land.

    The barrier between a man and a woman recurs in 'Givole Eshtaked' (Last Year's Stalks, 1903), which, like many of Bialik's poems, is preoccupied with imagery of fertility and infertility.[14] The growth and burning of the roses inside the poet's beloved might symbolize the menstrual cycle, uninterruped by fertilization:

Stalks of last year's roses
    still lean and cling
to the walls of your heart—
My beloved! Look: a new spring
    dances in the garden
among the flower-beds and trees!

And the spade already starts
    to turn the earth,
bed after bed;
soon new flowers will spring
    up and climb
the grids of the fence.

And the shears already start
    to leap from tree to tree,
and prune the plants—
My beloved! the withered ones
    will bite the dust,
the fresh ones will live.

Do you hear how the smell
    of the new green shoots
wafts with the smell of myrrh?
That's how the orchard grows,
        sucking, giving suck, living
with its countless plants.

Towards evening, the lovely innocent
    little girl,
the gardener's daughter, gathers up
the cutting of the shears—and at night
        last year's stalks
go up in fire.

Other poems written during the same period as the 'Poems of
Wrath' continue the grief-stricken confession of emotional
deprivation. In the poems 'Ayekh?' (Where Are You?) and
'Ve-Im yishal ha-malakh' (And if the angel should ask), both
dating from 1904 when Bialik was in Warsaw, the longing for
woman and the search for love are bound up with the yearning
for the lost world of wholeness in Jewish tradition. Here is the
end of 'Ayekh?':

... All day long, between
letters of the Talmud, in a shaft of light
a bright cloud, in my prayers and my purest
thought, in my bitter suffering—I searched
only for you, only you,
you, you ...

In 'Ve-Im yishal ha-malakh' the search continues. Bialik placed
this poem after 'Davar' in the 1923 edition of his collected works,
and it has remained there ever since. Perhaps no two poems by
Bialik are more dissimilar: one gives voice to a powerful
prophet, the other is spoken by a wounded child. Yet the poems
express two sides of the same personality. As 'Davar' ends with
the angel of death, it may be that the angel with whom the poet
speaks in 'Ve-Im yishal ha-malakh' is also the angel of death. The
poet's spirit finds temporary refuge in the Talmud—the 'belly of
dead letters'—and is moved to sing:

> But one song she didn't know—
> a song of youth and love. She found
> no comfort, and she longed to get away.
> She felt squeezed almost to death.
> One day I looked at my worn Gemara—
> and she had flown away. And still she soars
> and wanders, and finds no comfort.
> At night, during the start of each month,
> when the world prays for the damaged moon,
> she clings with her wings to the gate
> of love, clings and knocks, she weeps
> in secret and prays
> for love ...

The poem 'Haknisini taḥat kenafekh' (Take me under your wing, 1905) was written shortly after Bialik returned to his wife after his year's absence in Warsaw:

> Take me under your wing,
> be my mother and sister,
> your breast my head's refuge
> nest of my outcast prayers.

This poem may be read as an exquisite miniature of *Megillat ha-Esh*, written later in the same year. The image of the idealized woman sexually out of reach recurs also in 'Holekhet at me-imi' (You're leaving me, 1907):

> Your memory, pure angel, goes with me,
> It shelters me like the grace of God,
> Whispering a blessing, trembling with restraint,
> Like a mother's tear falling on a Sabbath candle.

Bialik made no secret of the biographical basis of his poetry. In a long autobiographical letter to Joseph Klausner, written in Kishinev in 1903, he compared his writing to a flower growing from the soil of his experience.[15] Many of the love lyrics transparently express the longing for a mother-figure, or a woman who has inexplicably abandoned the poet. In this respect, the poems 'Be-Yom stav' and 'Predah' are a key to

Bialik's writings. The motif of orphanhood apparently links the love lyrics with the 'Poems of Wrath'. A child who loses his mother will often idealize her and search for idealized mother-substitutes, in objects as well as in people. The extreme of idealization may be treated as a gauge of the violent anger which he feels as a result of being 'abandoned', especially if his conditions for mourning are poor.[16] This inner violence may be terrifying, and the child may deal with it by splitting it off from the idealized image of woman. In Bialik's case, the unusually strong need for the mother he had lost at seven was apparently coupled with precisely such ungovernable wrath. He evidently treated his wife as a mother-substitute[17] and allegedly confessed that his wife 'suffered a great deal from my paroxysms of stormy rage'.[18] This anger might have found an outlet in the 'Poems of Wrath'. Only in *Megillat ha-Esh* did Bialik yoke together the emotional extremes of the 1903–6 period: that of the helpless child in need of love and of the wrathful prophet.

The Scroll of Fire

Megillat ha-Esh is the climax of Bialik's poetry, a long prose-poem in nine sections which effectively sums up all that he had written and was to write. The Yiddish writer Isaac Leib Peretz compared *Megillat ha-Esh* to a star that had exploded into fragments. The poem is a complex, occasionally obscure Romantic allegory of national and personal trauma, and scholars have been arguing over it since its publication in 1905. No summary of the poem can do justice to its richness. However, as it is central to an understanding of Bialik's work, and as it has a story, the story may be summed up briefly. The poem starts with a spectacular account of the destruction of the Second Temple in Jerusalem in 70 CE.

> All night seas of flame boiled and tongues
> of fire leaped about the Temple-mount. Stars flew
> from the charred heavens and fell to earth in
> showers of sparks. Did God kick his throne away
> and smash his crown?

The next morning the ministering angels find God in mourning among the ruins:

> He was cloaked in pillars of smoke
> and his footstool was dust and ashes.
> His head, buried in his arms, was covered
> by mountains of grief. Silent and desolate
> he sat and stared at the ruin. Wrath
> of eternity darkened his eyelids
> and the great silence was frozen in his eyes.

Bialik interweaves two *aggadot* on the *ḥurban* (destruction) of the Temple: that of the sacred fire saved from the ruined altar (II Maccabees 1: 19 ff.) and of the children who leap from the boat taking them to Rome in order to escape their fate (*Gittin* 57b).[19] An angel rescues the sacred fire and carries it to the top of a cliff on a desert island. The children are shipwrecked on this island. The boys, separated from the girls, wander for several days in search of water, but find that the island is completely desolate and bare. They arrive at a river which, in Bialik's allegory, represents corruption. By this time, two conflicting attitudes have emerged among the boys, represented by two different characters: Wrath and Hope. The character representing Wrath speaks lines which could come from one of Bialik's 'Poems of Wrath':

> From the depth of destruction raise a song of ruin
> Black like the brand of your heart;
> Bear it among the nations, scatter it with the wrath of God,
> Empty its coals over their heads.

The character representing Hope is the only one who does not drink from the river. His attempt to console the others fails. The song of Wrath gathers strength. At this moment, the girls appear on top of the cliff on the bank opposite. They march as if hypnotized and leap one by one into the river. All the boys except for the one representing Hope leap in after them. The river swallows them all. One girl remains at the top of the cliff, and the survivor recognizes her. His confession to her, the heart of the poem, is similar to Bialik's other love poems, and it brings to mind the Song of Songs. The boy tells of the death of his father, when his mother was unable to raise him. Among the hills of Samaria, he had first seen his beloved. As in Bialik's other lyrics, his feelings towards her are those of a helpless child towards his mother:

> All my life my soul cried out to you in a
> thousand voices, and in tens of thousands of ways,
> crooked and invisible, fled from you to you . . .
> Even as a baby in the black of night, I saw
> your beauty and coveted your hidden light . . .
> With the sorrow of a mother the golden light
> of your eye rested on me . . . at night
> like a weaned child on his mother's lap
> I made my love known and I waited.

A Nazirite (reminiscent both of Bialik's grandfather and of the head of the Volozhin yeshivah) raises him, but he does not forget his beloved. As he grows older, the fire of lust within him conflicts with his inner religious fire. Eventually, he himself becomes a Nazirite in the Temple in Jerusalem. But, he declares, now that the Temple is no more, he is ready to dedicate himself to his beloved. He looks up and finds that the girl has disappeared. Only her reflection remains in the river.[20] Following the reflection, he climbs a steep cliff where he finds the sacred fire. He lifts it up in triumph, intending to devote himself again to the worship of God. At this moment, he looks down. Consumed by the fire of lust and clutching the sacred fire, he falls into the arms of the girl reflected in the river. He is carried to a distant land of exile. Here he becomes a prophetic figure, expressing the pain and wrath of the exiles, but intermingled with this is the pain of unsatisfied love. At times he is overwhelmed by purely personal suffering (*yegon ha-yaḥid*). The poem ends with the angel who has tried to save the sacred fire removing tears, apparently those of the fallen prophet, from the cup of national sorrows:[21]

The young sad-eyed angel, pure of wing
standing over the morning star, tipped silently
the dumb cup of sorrow—and emptied tear after tear
in the silence of the dawn.

The immediate event behind *Megillat ha-Esh* was the naval mutiny in June 1905 when Odessa was shelled for several days by the sailors on board the battleship *Potemkin* (the event depicted unforgettably in Eisenstein's film). Bialik was there when the oil refineries were hit and the entire harbour was set ablaze. In February 1933 he gave a public speech on *Megillat ha-Esh* in Tel Aviv in which he recalled the electric atmosphere in Odessa at the time: 'The daily cannon fire and gun shots stirred up a storm in me.'[22] However, he admitted, there were private reasons for writing the poem which he could not discuss publicly.

We now know that during the time of writing *Megillat ha-Esh*, Bialik was involved with a Russian-Jewish artist, Ira Jahn (Slyapin), for whom he wrote the poems 'Holekhet at me-imi' and 'Li-Netivekh ha-ne'elam' (In your vanished traces, 1907?) (It is of psychological interest that both poems are concerned with the separation of the poet from his beloved.) In a letter that he sent Ira Jahn after completing *Megillat ha-Esh* in the summer of 1905, he wrote: 'Immediately after you left my spirits dropped. I couldn't finish the poem. I thought I would go mad.'[23]

Similarly, the account of the burning Temple with which the poem begins was apparently influenced less by the classical sources than by a childhood memory of a fire dating from the time after the death of the poet's father in Zhitomir, when he was about seven and a half:

This was the first fire I had ever seen. No later fire, even much bigger ones, ever made such an impression. In the middle of that night it seemed the whole world was being destroyed. Everything was lit up—I saw a plain, a field, a synagogue—I heard cries—it was all a game, an entertainment. I remember I was very happy at the sight, but there was also the fear of God. When I wrote the opening of *Megillat ha-Esh* I recalled the dry trees burning fiercely in a storm of fire. Everything was wiped out, only heaps of coals remained.[24]

This memory might be interpreted as a 'screen memory', both revealing and disguising a whole aspect of Bialik's life.[25] A child who has just lost his father and is about to be separated from his mother, as Bialik was at the time of the fire, might well feel that 'the whole world was being destroyed'. At its deepest personal level, *Megillat ha-Esh* is a confession of the effects of loss, the sense of ruin, depression and anger, and the distorted sexual relationships which followed. The ambivalence of the central character towards his 'prophetic' role—his guilty awareness of private as well as national motivations—is a key to the poem and to Bialik's career as a whole. However, a full discussion of this ambivalence, in *Megillat ha-Esh* and elsewhere in Bialik's writings, must wait until the next chapter.

After *Megillat ha-Esh*, Bialik's poetry became increasingly pessimistic, to the point of suicidal despair, the extremity of which has few precedents in literature and which goes against the main current of Jewish tradition, with its fundamental optimism. At times it is possible to ascribe concrete causes to the raw misery which fills Bialik's poetry at this time, for example in 'Yadati be-lel arafel' which on one level is a response to the pogroms of 1905. The politics of Zionism were also dispiriting, invariably. The poem 'Al levavkhem she-shamen' (On your desolate hearts, 1897) had its initial inspiration in the First Zionist Congress of 1897:

> Do you see who lurks
>   behind the door, broom in hand?
> The caretaker of ruined temples—
> Despair!

Another poem of despair, 'Hem mitna'arim me'afar' (They shake the dust, 1907), was written after the 8th Congress, held in The Hague in 1907. This was the first Congress in which Bialik participated, as a representative of the Odessa Zionists. As in other poems, notably *Megillat ha-Esh*, his response to public crisis

was coloured by possibly unconscious associations with childhood trauma, symbolized by the ruined Temple, abandoned
by God and deeply mourned. In its possession by death, the
poem brings to mind some of the Metaphysical and Jacobean
poets, such as Donne and Webster. The macabre complex of
emotions and attitudes which fills the poem—grief, disgrace,
rage, judgement—is synthesized in a harsh, pathos-laden utter-
ance:

I

They shake the dust
    off themselves
Already, they rise from mourning—
And I,
Shoeless, ashes on my head
    will sit waiting, in silence.

Silently I'll sit, facing
    their dumb temple,
Not a prayer in me—
For whom, over what?
Their temple stands
    but God has left.

Heavy grief darkens in me—
    they go on
innocently.
And I, shoeless
will mourn in solitude
    waiting, in silence—

2

And if I die, devoured
    by rage
at the ruin of your temple,
let me die in silence; don't disturb
my bones, don't profane my memory
    with tears of deceit.

There's seven levels in hell—
    in my life
they've all burned me, they will again
when I die. Roast my heart, scatter
my ashes, but don't judge me,
    not with your scalding tear.

And if I rot in the grave—
    let me surely rot,
to dream your rottenness;
eaten by worms, my skeleton
will laugh at your calamity
    shudder at your disgrace.

Another, interconnected, cause of the poet's despair is the subject of the poem 'Lifne Aron ha-Sefarim': the poet's inability to find comfort in his childhood world of tradition and observance. Symbol of this world is the bookcase, its books, once revered as sacred Torah, now infested with mice. The poet is caught between two worlds, one dead, the other as yet unborn. Attempting to return to the dead world of the *matmid* that he once was, the poet finds none of the consolatory faith to which the *matmid* dedicates his life. Instead, he recalls the time when he lost his faith: 'I saw my fortress ruined. The *Shekhinah*[26] I saw stealing from the Holy Ark, and the image of my grandfather, shadowing my conscience, a witness and a silent judge—he, too, vanished.' Now he returns to the rotten volumes of his youth, as if to dead trees, digging frantically for signs of life. Emerging into the night, he sees no light of faith, but what Matthew Arnold, in 'Dover Beach', describes as

    the vast edges drear
And naked shingles of the world.

The poet, in despair, calls Night to gather him up, into the eternal peace of the dark.

Bialik's visit to Palestine in 1909, his full awakening to the gap between what he was perceived to be and what he knew himself to be, his recognition of the poverty of the Land of Israel and of the Zionist movement, might also have contributed to his pessimism. Curiously, there is not a single direct reference to the Land of Israel in any of the poems of this period.[27]

Public crises and disasters alone, however, do not account for the extreme, persistent streak of despair in Bialik, especially in the poems of 1906–11. In the poem 'Al-kef yam-mavet zeh', for example, the poet's sense of ruin and desolation is clearly linked to the departure from Odessa of Ahad Ha'am, to whom the poem is dedicated. But the poem can also be read in the light of poems of Bialik's childhood loss, such as 'Be-Yom stav' or *Yatmut*. The loss of his father and separation from his mother as a child had inclined Bialik to depression, guilt and anger, all of which underlie his poetry of despair.[28] We are told by Ravnitzky that Bialik had suicidal impulses while living with his grandparents after his father's death.[29] The poet's depression and despair over parting from his mother at this time apparently set the pattern for his reactions to separations in later life. The poems 'Li-Netivekh ha-ne'elam', 'Holekhet at me-imi' and 'Arvit' (Evening, 1908), in common with earlier poems such as 'Be-Yom stav', 'Ayekh?' and *Megillat ha-Esh*, convey the poet's grief on being separated from a beloved woman. Here is 'Arvit':

> The sun rose, the sun also set—
> but she was gone,
> another day, two days—not a sign
> anywhere.
>
> The west fills up with shapeless forms,
> clouds on the horizon—
> are worlds being built, do you know,
> or destroyed?
>
> No, neither built nor destroyed,
> I see:
> This epicene dusk scatters ashes
> everywhere.
>
> One thing more: I sought your change
> and lost my gold—
> and the devil stands behind me, laughing
> cruelly.

During the previous year, in 1907, Bialik had written to his friend Ben-Ami of his suicidal urges: 'Sometimes I feel like commiting suicide—and I am too idle to do this good thing . . . What difference if I live?'[30] In one of the more morbid poems of this period, 'Lo herani Elohim' (God did not show me, 1911), the poet gives expression to his wish for death:

> . . . perhaps through my very hunger and thirst for life and its beauty, with disgusted soul, braving the fury of the Creator, I will kick at his gift and cast my life at his feet, like a defiled shoe torn from the foot . . .

Again and again in this extraordinary series of poems, the poet appears to reject his public role and reiterates his feelings of guilt and unworthiness in the face of the massive burden thrust upon him. In a confessional vein he wrote to Simon Dubnow: '"Fame imposes obligations." This shakes me to the bone. I do not like duty, obligations. If a hollow reed like me has been chosen by the Almighty to be his flute—what am I and what is my strength?'[31] 'Mi ani u-mah ani' (Who am I, 1911) is a poetic expression of this sense of inadequacy culminating in a death-wish:

> Who am I and what am I
>   that a golden ray should welcome me
> And a breeze, tender-winged
>   should grace my cheek?
> What does it matter if the corn
>   clings to me in the field
> Or fresh grass kisses my feet?
> The Lord's blessing is late,
> His mercy slow in coming
> There's no longer room in me
> Let them find another place, and alone
> I'll return to my silence
> I'll ask nothing more than a stone
>   for a pillow
> A stone from a ruin, unwanted, useless,
>   all spark of life gone

I'll hug it, I'll join myself to it
I'll shut my eyes, and petrify—
Let me have no dream or vision
    no memory or hope
No yesterday, no tomorrow
But everything frozen, eternal silence, unbroken
    to swallow me up
No leaf will shiver for me
    no grass will mourn
No path to cross my border
No ray of light to see me
And the song of a bird will die
        at my feet—
Only a little cloud will waver above me
        for an instant
watching—and float silently on.

The poem 'Ve-Haya ki timtze'u' seems also to be addressed to the reader who wishes to know how to read Bialik and what to make of him:

And if you find the scroll of my heart
Rolling in the dust,
                    Say this:
There was a man
pure, simple, tired, weak.

And this man lived innocently
    he shied away
in silence he took
    —with neither blessing nor curse—
whatever came.

And the man went out in innocence,
he didn't go a stubborn way;
    from petty things he didn't run
        and greatness he didn't hope,
            and what was hidden he didn't seek.

And if greatness came,
   late, unwanted—on the king's highway
he'd stand and watch, astonished
and bow his head, and move on.

And if what was hidden came,
   late, knocking on his door
he would not take it in,
despising as one the insolent greed
     of the dogs
and the rabbit's righteous heart.

And this man had a little attic
with a tiny window
his alone, he knew no angel in it
   no demon ruled it.

In time of trouble
he had one prayer
he would go up there
    and sink down
before the window
    trembling, burning—
praying in silence.

And the prayer lasted his life
but God didn't want it.
What he didn't want was given him,
and the one thing he asked—
    he didn't find.

Till his last day this man
never lost hope of mercy,
heart and soul he prayed,
    prayed and died
in the middle of prayer.

   Yet another lyric confessing the nature of the poet's character and creativity is 'Vi-Yhi mi ha-ish' (Whoever be the man, 1911):

Whoever be the man who follows me,
Freer than I, straighter,
His life ten times better than mine,
Whether or not he understands what I have said—
I'll be sure of one thing:
He will not scorn my heart's turmoil,
Nor mock the pain of my soul.
Alone, wherever he may be,
      he'll sink himself
into the ragged book of my life,
Drink in all the bitter words
They'll pour into his bones
           like flaming tar—
Drive him mad, screaming
Roasted alive on his coals.
When he can no longer drag
  his soul between the lines,
Paths of fire, snow, blood-stained—
When he recoils from the scorpion words
Stinging themselves in bitterness,
Biting, gnashing, poisoning
Strangled by the will to rebel, powerless
Soaked in fury, cursing the cry
    of father and mother
And the name of their God—
He will turn aside, and see my soul
Standing in silence by the door
Exposed in all its flaws and afflictions,
      its failings and shame:
'Look, here I am, this was my life,
my strength, my faith and bitterness.'
And the momentary spark
of disdain in his eyes
             will go out
His rebuke will die on his lips;
And tears will come, in secret
To redeem the shame of my life
And atone for the disgrace
    of my affliction.

The final lyric of the 1906–11 period is also one of Bialik's most celebrated: 'Tzanaḥ lo zalzal' (Like a fallen branch, 1911). This poem marks the end of the most important phase of Bialik's career as a poet and the start of the *shtika*:

> Like a fallen branch across a gate
> sleep comes to me:
> My fruit has fallen, what use
> my branch or tree?
>
> The fruit's fallen, blossom forgotten—
> leaves remain—
> one troubled night they'll fall
> earthwards slain.
>
> After—more dreadful nights alone,
> no sleep or rest at all.
> I'll bang myself against the dark,
> smash my head on the wall.
>
> Spring will sprout again, and I,
> upon my bough I'll hang in grief—
> a sceptre bald, no flower his, nor blossom
> no fruit, no leaf.

One of the mysteries of modern literature is why Bialik at the height of his powers should have practically abandoned poetry after writing 'Tzanaḥ lo zalzal'. (The *Poems* include only ten poems between 1911 and Bialik's death in 1934, if we count *Yatmut* as one poem.) Some have suggested that he despaired of helping his people, or that, with an almost maniacally intense period of creativity, he had burned himself out. It may be that, as in the case of Wordsworth and other poets, as he approached middle age his inspiration deserted him.[32] The difference in stress in Palestinian and European use of Hebrew may have discouraged him. Perhaps he had said all that he had to say, or, as he became established as a public figure, no longer felt the need to write. There were also practical reasons for the decline in his poetic output. His business affairs and his public role occupied him increasingly during the pre-1914 years. Poems such as

'Vi-Yhi mi ha-ish' were not what the public expected of a National Poet.

Perhaps most important, there were emotional causes, the exact nature of which is obscure. To Jacob Fichman, Bialik described the silence which had overwhelmed him during the last months of 1909 as 'a form of sickness, the nature of which I don't understand'.[33] In a confession of his state of mind just before the *shtika* began, he wrote to his friend S. Ben Zion in tones reminiscent of 'Tzanah lo zalzal': 'Sometimes I think I'm going mad. I lack nothing, it seems, but I have no peace of mind. What is it? I don't know. Big and little sins gnaw at me like worms. At night I don't sleep. I'm worn out by ugly idleness, and I feel that I'm wallowing in a filthy pit.'[34]

The following year, in the summer of 1912, Bialik's house in Odessa was burgled. A young acquaintance, Nathan Goren, went with him to the police. Goren, who had adulated Bialik as National Poet, now saw a side of him that he never expected. The poet sobbed out his anguish at being unable to write. Though he had tried, he had not a spark of creativity in him: 'He simply couldn't write. It was terrible. A man runs around with his eyes closed, not knowing where he's going. He's ashamed to admit that for months he had left letters unanswered. His fingers didn't move. He feels as though a heavy black block has dropped on him, squashing, strangling him, without his feeling it.'[35]

No one to my knowledge has suggested a connection between Bialik's *shtika* and the death of his mother which occurred during this period. This loss, which is passed over in complete silence in his writings, may well have been one of the key events of his inner life. His mother had moved to Odessa and lived with the poet and his wife during her last three years. Her gloomy presence was remarked upon by a number of Bialik's friends: Ravnitzky described her as lying on a couch for days, groaning in misery.[36] The increasing pessimism of Bialik's poetry during the years up to 1911 might well have been affected by his mother's dying. It may be that he connected her death with her separation from him when he was a child, and the anxiety, anger and depression which he felt after losing her the first time may have been revived by her death. As he had not mourned her fully as a child, his grief and despair, the 'heavy black block', were almost unbearable at times. They might have stifled his creativity. Though he would write outstanding poetry after 'Tzanaḥ lo zalzal'—notably the poems of 1915–16, the first chapter of *Safiaḥ* and *Yatmut*—he would never again be struck by lightning as he had been during the great years.

Aftergrowth

After leaving Russia in 1921, Bialik wrote one of his finest, most sustained pieces of imaginative prose—the opening chapter of *Safiaḥ*, his *aggadic* autobiography. He had worked on *Safiaḥ* periodically since the turn of the century: two major fragments of the work had already been published, in 1908 (ch. 2–8) and 1919 (ch. 9–15). The 1908 chapters consist of a series of charming vignettes of the poet's life at home and in school in the idyllic setting of Radi in the 1870s. The child's imagination develops in spite—or because—of the unfavourable environment: a father who beats him, a mother who neglects him, teachers who abuse and degrade him. He finds in himself an almost phenomenal capacity for concentration, for thrusting himself body and soul into everything he sees and does. His imagination helps to compensate for his emotional handicaps—loneliness and a lack of sympathy and understanding. He transforms simple objects, a mirror, a group of marbles, the stove, the kitchen wall, the letters of the Hebrew alphabet, into a new world which he alone can enter. The kitchen wall, for example, though ugly and unpromising, contains everything the child wants:

> The lower half of this wall was damp and mildewed and exuded a sort of green sweat. It had long attracted my attention. On rainy days I would sit facing it for hours on end, gazing at the queer shapes which the moisture scrawled upon it. In the green stains I saw whatever the eye might desire: mountains and valleys, fields and forests, castles and palaces. Such a wall, I told myself, must have been expressly created for milking; and I could no longer spend my spare time anywhere else... In the lower part of the wall, near the corner, I saw a swollen place that looked

like a nipple. That was obviously the right spot. The only thing necessary was to make a little hole and stick in a tube and milk would promptly gush forth like an overflowing fountain.[37]

The 1919 chapters continue the child's-eye view of his own growth, this time in more congenial surroundings, the *heder* of a kind and sympathetic rabbi. His imagination free to roam, the child 'enters' the *aggadic* world to which he is constantly exposed in daily studies and participates in the living myths of Jewish tradition. He does not just learn about the ancient Israelites: he becomes one:

> By day we crossed the desert, a land of drouth and thirst, the dwelling place of serpent, basilisk and scorpion. The young men paced at the flanks of their camels which were laden with rolls upon rolls of silk, satin, fabrics, purple and scarlet, and bundles upon bundles of powders, lotus, balsam and all the many spices. And the elders, white of beard and wearing their turbans, rode ahead resplendently garbed and honourable, upon white she-asses, their feet in hose and sandals all but touching the ground and scooping fine faint tracks in the sand.
>
> At night we would stop to rest in the woods. There we would light the campfires and sleep around them on the ground, completely surrounded by a barricade of stones fashioned with an outward-curving edge, a tried barrier against wild beasts, as was done, says Rashi, by our father Jacob.[38]

The opening chapter of *Safiah*, which came out in 1923, was written about three years later. In the meantime, Bialik had lost everything in Russia (including a library of 3000 books) and was having much difficulty in re-establishing his life and career in post-war Germany. In Berlin in 1922 he wrote to an acquaintance that 'the city in which I'm living is foreign to me. I don't know its ways, and the people among whom I live are an exiled, wandering people who don't know what the next day will bring.'[39] In this time of crisis he looked back to his early childhood with especially strong feeling. *Safiaḥ* ch. 1 is an ecstatic prose-poem, a Wordsworthian paean to childhood. It reveals a side of Bialik which he had hinted at in earlier poems, such as 'Zohar' (Splendour, 1900), but never so strongly. For there was a deep mystical strain in Bialik. His childhood as he depicts it was infused with the passion for revelation, a conviction of being in touch with a higher unknown power. Here as elsewhere in *Safiaḥ* there are more than a few hints that the child's mystical apprehension of the universe was a means of escape from deprivation, abandonment and depression. Yet Bialik is concerned less with trauma than with the creative offshoots of trauma, the birth of his gifts, his delight in the mystery of creation around him. Alluding to the Psalms, 'For my father and mother have forsaken me, but the Lord will take me up' (27: 10), Bialik confesses that he perceives Nature as one huge *aggadah* prepared for his delight by the divine parent:

> Like a forsaken fledgling I wandered alone about my nest; my father and mother had forsaken me and there was no one else to look after me. Then God in His mercy took me under the shelter of His wings ... His hidden hand sowed my paths with wonders and placed riddles in everything, upon which my eye alighted. Every stone and pebble, every splinter of wood was an inexplicable text, and in every ditch and hollow eternal secrets lurked.[40]

In rhetoric reminiscent of the closing chapters of the book of Job, but in a tone of wonder rather than of accusation, the poet revives his pristine sense of the mystery of creation, the soul of poetry:

> How can a spark be contained in a mute stone, and who puts the dumb shadows on the house walls? Who heaps up the fiery mountains in the skirts of heaven, and who holds the moon in the thickets of the forest? Whither stream the caravans of clouds, and whom does the wind in the field pursue? Why does my flesh sing in the morning, and what is the yearning in my heart at evening time? What is wrong with the waters of the spring that they weep

quietly, and why does my heart leap at the sound? These
wonders were all about me, caught me up, passed over my
poor little head—and refuge and escape there was none.
They widened my eyes and deepened my heart, until I
could sense mysteries everywhere.[41]

The sense of wonder and the mystery of childhood emerge also
in Bialik's legends and poems for children, for whom most of his
creative writing after 'Tzanaḥ lo zalzal' was intended. The poems
were collected in 1933 in *Shirim u-Fizmonot li-Ladim* and the
legends in 1934, in *Va-Yhi ha-Yom*. The legends are embel-
lished retellings of traditional folk tales, mostly concerning
King David and King Solomon in the Talmudic and Midrashic
aggadah. This work is of extremely high literary quality, notably
Aggadat Shelosha ve-Arba'ah (The Legend of Three and Four,
1929) which ranks with Bialik's finest prose works: it is possible
to feel that he poured into it the love he wanted to give to
children of his own. Some of these tales are full of the exuberance
of childhood. In the poems, which are simple, touching and
amusing, Bialik shows his mastery of the music and rhythm of
Hebrew: a knowledge of the language is unnecessary in order to
respond to the words. Here is a swing:

> Nad ned nad ned
> red aleh aleh va–red;

here is a galloping horse:

> Rutz ben susi rutz u-dehar
> Tus ba-givah tus ba-har;

and here is a butterfly in flight:

> Parpar parpar peraḥ ḥai
> Red na maher shev alai.

However, in other works for children Bialik gave vent to
feelings which he might not have wished to express so clearly in
his poems for grown-ups. The legend 'Sefer Bereshit' (The Book
of Genesis, 1926–7), for example, begins with a description of the
pain and frustration of childlessness:

Once there was a man, just and righteous and pure, and the Lord gave him wealth and much property, but he didn't give him children. And the man was old and sad and deeply distressed, and he said, 'What's the use of all my wealth if I have no son to revive my spirits in old age and to bear my name after my death?' He and his wife pined and prayed to God each day and cried for children. And when he went to the synagogue and heard the children chattering and reciting in school, his heart would well up with longing and his soul would go out to them.[42]

This man's daily prayer for children brings to mind the man in 'Ve-Haya ki timtze'u', and his constant prayer for something that he never gets.

Nor was the poetry for children an escape. Longing and deprivation permeate many of these poems:

> How shall I enter the gates
> of the treasured land,
> if my key is broken
> and the door is locked?
> 'Me-Aḥore ha-Sha'ar' (Behind the Gate, 1926–7)

> In a corner, widower and orphan—
> a pale *lulav*, an *etrog** with cut stem.
> ... My garden is ruined, its stalks crushed,
> its ways untrodden
> 'Avim Ḥoshrim' (Cloud Darken, 1920s?)

> How can I rejoice,
> how can I dance—
> My blossoms have fallen,
> my pods are empty.
> 'Be-Ginat ha-Yarak' (In the Vegetable Garden,
> 1933)

---

* *lulav* = palm branch; *etrog* = citron. Both are used in the celebration of *Sukkot*.

Orphanhood

Apart from the children's poems, Bialik's major poetic work of the last quarter-century of his life was *Yatmut*, which may be read as his literary testament. Totally lacking in 'national' significance, it acts as a signpost for critics who, rather than use Bialik for propaganda, truthfully wish to comprehend the personal sources of his artistic motivation. The first of the four poems which make up *Yatmut* is 'Avi',[43] which was written in 1928, apparently as an independent poem. 'Avi' is a wrenching portrait of Bialik's father as he remembered him shortly before his death:

> ... a weary ox, broad-boned, bearing its yoke, trudging heavily in silence, wretched and restrained, the same image in all seasons: he walks in anger, dragging his life-cart, heavy with stones, through paths thick with mud or sand or clouds of dust, through days pelting or burning in anger, neck bent by the yoke, forehead furrowed with worry, his eyes—wells of sorrow, contemplating against all hope, at every crossroad, at each new road: will someone ever help me?

If the father's death was hard to confront squarely, the separation from the mother was the most delicate, conflict-ridden subject Bialik could face. He waited five years before writing what became the second and third poems in the cycle, 'Shiva' (Mourning) and 'Almenut' (Widowhood) in 1933. These poems depict the family's mourning immediately after the death and the reduced circumstances which forced the separation from the mother. Bialik goes so far out of his way to assert his mother's innocence as to suggest that at the time he had to make a powerful effort to believe it. The neighbours gossiped maliciously about the raven-like mother who cruelly sent her young from the nest. In reply, the poet describes the torment which led up to the mother's decision, the sleepless nights, the prayers and tears, the family heirlooms pawned:

> ... perhaps you will imagine, as I do, what my mother felt that bitter evening before our separation, when she

embraced me, agitated, bewildered, laughing and crying, what she asked when she looked deep into my eyes, as if digging into their depths to uncover their judgement, kissing me over and over, crying—what a struggle it was for her to find the words to tell me, halting, crying, that she wasn't strong enough and she had no choice but to bring me to the home of her father-in-law.

Bialik describes his mother's feelings, as he remembers or imagines them, not his own. But in 'Predah', the final section of *Yatmut* and the last poem he wrote, he hints that although he did not grasp the full meaning of the loss of his mother, he did hold it against her. The consolation which he offers to her, whether intended or not, is faintly ironic:

Don't sorrow for having sent me away, tomorrow is the eve of the new month, you'll visit father's grave and tell him all your suffering and affliction—he will understand, he will believe it, and he will forgive you.

The implication here is, perhaps, that while the dead father could understand, believe and forgive, the child himself could not. Such a reaction would not be unusual for a child of seven.[44] Yet 'Predah' is not just a farewell to the poet's lost childhood but also to his art and to life itself. The poem quivers with heartbreak and, like some of the slow movements in the symphonies of Gustav Mahler, treads perilously on the border of sentimentality and self-pity. 'Predah' and the other poems in *Yatmut* are saved from these pitfalls by a finely judged ambiguity of perspective. The breakdown of the family is seen through the eyes of the child, yet the poet is a sixty-year-old public man studying his memories, weighing them on the balance of his life and work, judging himself and his family. The end of 'Predah' is a masterly piece of naïve art. The poet does not intrude on the child's superficial impressions, but merely records them, with wonderful pathos, in all their simplicity and innocence. The poet and his mother are just entering Zhitomir. She will say goodbye and leave him with his grandparents. These are the last lines Bialik wrote:

...I looked up in astonishment and saw the giant houses on either side, I was moving between walls in an enormous city. The houses were like palaces, one bigger than the other, and I was so small, like a grasshopper. I liked the city, I was drawn to it, as it still had the bright, fresh look of morning. Mother took me through streets and back-streets, alleys and market-places, and my eyes wandered, astonished. Finally we emerged in open spaces of gardens and fenced enclosures; and I was full of new, secret things, and alternately tired. By noon we arrived at my old grandfather's house in the timber-merchants' suburb on the other side of town.

Bialik ends his life as a poet with the implied irony that the child that he was, with his vivid sense of the present, had not fully understood his tragedy. He does not yet see into the nature of things, as the poet in later life is compelled to do. This is not yet a separation, a form of death, but a deceptive prelude to bitterness and fury, to a life whose artistic expression is compared by the poet, with the benefit of hindsight, to a scroll in the dust.

5

NATIONAL FIGURE

Bialik's lasting importance as a poet rests on about two dozen lyrics and 'Poems of Wrath' which place him in the company of the great nineteenth-century Romantics, such as Wordsworth and Schiller—the only modern Hebrew poet who unhesitatingly warrants such comparison. Most of these poems have little, if anything, to do with Jewish nationalism. Bialik's distinctive 'national' poems were mostly written before he reached his full poetic powers. 'Birkhat Am', for example, was written in 1894 in praise of the pioneers in the Land of Israel. Its first stanza became an anthem of the Zionist movement:

> May the hands of our brethren who grace the dust of our land, wherever they are, be strengthened; let not your spirit fail—joyful, singing, come in force to the help of the nation!

'Mete Midbar ha-Aḥaronim' (The Last Dead of the Wilderness), written about two years later, is also a call for national revival. It alludes to the *aggadic* theme which Bialik was to develop more elaborately and ambiguously in 'Mete Midbar'. Its impact was even greater than that of 'Birkhat Am', but again its importance is more historical than aesthetic:

> Rise, desert wanderers, leave the wilderness,
> Far is the way, many the battles . . .

'La-Mitnadvim ba-Am', dating from 1899, is a fervid appeal for aid for the national cause:

> To the nation's help! To the nation's help! With what?
> Don't ask—with whatever we find! With whom? Don't
> check—whoever gives himself! Whoever is touched by

nation's trouble. When the camp gathers, do not exclude him! All offers accepted, all gifts are good, no time to check in time of peril!

Though these poems are more impressive in Hebrew than in translation—the quality of the Hebrew and the poetic spirit are remarkable in so young a poet—they are hardly among Bialik's finest works. Yet they appear to have set the tone for Bialik's acclaim as the national poet of the Jewish people. Chaim Weizmann expressed a commonly held view when he described Bialik as 'a giant of the Zionist movement'.[1] Bialik's friend Chaim Chernowitz (Rav Tzair), who had known him for many years in Odessa, wrote of him as a spiritual exegete, the 'Rashi of Zionism'.[2] Were these misnomers, the products of a misunderstanding?

Though he cared little for his national role, Bialik was a national poet in the fullest sense. His poetry would have been inconceivable without the Zionist movement. It was the outstanding literary product of the rise of Jewish nationalism and Hebrew in the 1880s and 1890s, which was, in turn, largely a reaction to the pogroms of 1881–4 and the defeated hopes of Russian-Jewish emancipation. Arriving at poetic maturity at the right moment, Bialik seized and was seized by the national cause, which by the turn of the century dominated Hebrew literature, and took his place on the empty pedestal of national poet. After 1903, when he wrote *Be-Ir ha-Haregah*, what he wrote was not as important as what he stood for: a new, aggressive, self-critical, forward-looking Jewish creativity.

Bialik's self-realization as a private lyric poet was, in a sense, a 'national' triumph. It was, however indirectly, proof of national identity on hostile soil, an assertion of pride in the creative use of Hebrew, the only national language of the Jewish people as a whole (in the orient as well as in Europe), of the possibilities of Jewish achievement in a new, evolving order. Yet his poetry was regarded by Bialik himself, and especially by others such as Ahad Ha'am, as pointing towards Zion, for only there, in Ahad Ha'am's view, could Hebrew literature survive in the long run. Mirrored in his poems are the desperate poverty and the anti-Semitism which drove the Russian Jews to emigration, socialism, revolution or Zionism. His poems of Zion, though again not among his best, are the finest in Hebrew since the time of Judah Halevi. These and the 'Poems of Wrath' in particular expressed a distinct national consciousness.

From today's perspective, the fact that Bialik wrote Hebrew poems of genius at a time when the Jews had no national territory of their own might seem little short of miraculous. Yet few national poets can have been better equipped for a more difficult task than Bialik. The Russian Jews, by virtue of their religious tradition and languages (Yiddish for everyday, Hebrew for prayer and study), their sufferings and hopes, had a stronger sense of collective destiny than any other Jewish community. This was why Zionism had its grass roots not in Western Europe but in the Pale of Settlement and why a national poet like Bialik was possible only in that violent godforsaken part of Russia. In social and religious background and education, fears, frustrations, outrage, Bialik was typical of many Russian Jews, and he spoke to his generation with particular authority and intensity.

Like many of his contemporaries, Bialik, before he abandoned his faith, had studied in a *heder*, in a *bet midrash* and in a yeshivah; in his youth he had read *Haskalah* writings in secret, as they were proscribed by the religious authorities; he had become involved in a clandestine Zionist group; his ambition throughout much of his early manhood was, in fact, to enrol in a modern rabbinical seminary and to further his Jewish education while acquiring a wider, secular knowledge. In his mature outlook, he embodied a wide variety of Jewish characteristics and trends, both traditional and modern: the grandeur and passion for justice of the Bible; the love for scriptural exposition and the legends and folklore of the Talmud; the religious fervour of his Hasidic upbringing; the intellectual discipline which he acquired in the *bet midrash* of Zhitomir and in the yeshivah of Volozhin (1886–91); the scientific scholarship of the *Wissenschaft des Judentums*; the thirst for secular knowledge characteristic of the *Haskalah* movement; the cultural Zionist nationalist philosophy of Ahad Ha'am; the artistic integrity and dedication of Mendele Mokher Sefarim.

It was natural for Bialik, given the circumstances of the times, to try to harness his gifts to the national cause, though this cause was, in fact, followed and sustained by only a tiny minority of the Russian Jews. For some, Zionism had taken the place of traditional Jewish faith and custom. Bialik was the first to give real artistic expression to the crisis of faith which he had himself experienced in moving from the comforting yet narrow and almost medieval world of the *shtetl* into the secular modern world.

As a public figure—though not as a poet—Bialik could offer a solution to the spiritual vacuum created by the decline of orthodox Jewish faith. In his speech at the dedication of the Hebrew University in 1925, he echoed Ahad Ha'am in describing the Jewish pioneers in the Land of Israel as fulfilling a religious task. Zionism was not a secular revolution, alien and antithetical to Judaism. Rather, Bialik implies, it was analogous to an almost incestuous reunion of sons with their lost motherland. (The Hebrew verb used here, *he-erah*, 'to spill', can mean, among other things, 'to have carnal knowledge'.) In creating the proverbial earthly Jerusalem, the pioneers were continuing the religious tradition and enabling the Jerusalem of the spirit to be built. In contrast with Bialik's poetry, *Megillat ha-Esh* for example, in which the sacred fire is defiled and lost, the fire of tradition may be handed on to the secular pioneers:

> Thousands of our young sons, responding to the call of their heart, stream to this land from all corners of the earth to redeem it from its desolation and ruin. They are ready to spill out their longing and strength into the bosom of this dry land in order to bring it to life. They plough through rocks, drain swamps, pave roads, singing with joy. These youngsters elevate crude physical labour to the level of supreme holiness, to the status of a religion. We must now light this holy flame within the walls of the building which is now being opened on Mount Scopus. Let these youngsters build with fire the lower Jerusalem while we build the higher Jerusalem. Our existence will be recreated and made secure by means of both ways together.[3]

Apart from the poems of Zion and the 'Poems of Wrath', a number of Bialik's other works bear a distinctly national character. He wrote the first folk poems in Hebrew: the piquancy of writing folk poems in a language that at the time (*c.* 1910) was hardly spoken did not escape him. His translations betray his national preoccupations. *Don Quixote* (1912, 1923) in Bialik's Hebrew can be read as his tribute to a national epic and as an allegory of Zionist aspirations, in the fashion of Mendele's classic *Masot Binyamin ha-Shlishi* (The Travels of Benjamin the Third, 1896), which was largely inspired by Cervantes. (Bialik's delightful experiment in rhymed narrative, *Aluf Batzlut ve-Aluf Shum*, is written in a similarly comic, bittersweet vein.) His translation of Schiller's *Wilhelm Tell*, too, is what one would expect of the poet of a rising national movement. Bialik was drawn to Schiller's play depicting the exploits of the great Swiss national hero and his victory over the hated tyrant Gessler, and his own hopes for Jewish nationalism and for Russia after the deposition of the hated Tsarist regime are reflected in his translation. *The Dybbuk*, the most famous play in Yiddish, attracted Bialik for somewhat similar reasons. He was convinced that national consciousness was built largely on archetypal legends and superstitions, and Ansky's play hauntingly explored some of these.

Bialik's concept of *kinnus*—the 'ingathering' of Jewish culture and its centralization in the Land of Israel—was also what one would expect of a Jewish national poet. His labours for *kinnus*—the co-editing of the *Sefer ha-Aggadah* and of medieval Hebrew poets, and his publication of a wide variety of Jewish writings through the ages—show him to have been a true ideological disciple of Ahad Ha'am. If Ahad Ha'am had laid down the 'Torah' of cultural Zionism, Bialik as the chief instigator of *kinnus* was, indeed, the 'Rashi' of Zionism. Again and again in his essays and speeches he returns to one of the central criticisms of the Jewish people voiced by Ahad Ha'am: if the Jews had not scattered their genius among the nations, but had used it in their own national cause, they would not be so enmired and degraded in the Diaspora. Rather, they would live in dignity and security in their own land, possess a brilliant culture and be 'a light unto the nations'.

As a public figure, too, Bialik was every inch the national poet. He became one of the best-known personalities in the Zionist movement, frequently attending the congresses and going on fund-raising missions. Especially during his final years, in Tel Aviv (1924–34), he was involved in all sorts of public and philanthropic activities. He had mass appeal to a degree unknown among Hebrew poets before or since. A public appearance of his might attract audiences of as many as five or ten thousand. Much of his writing consisted of public speeches, on such occasions as the opening of the Hebrew University in 1925, or eulogies on the deaths of prominent persons, such as Ahad Ha'am in 1927. On the surface, at any rate, he was very much a poet of the people, gregarious and highly approachable. Young authors came to him in droves for advice and help. For example, when the young Gershom Scholem embarked on his lifelong study of Jewish mysticism, the Kabbalah, he first sought Bialik's approval and support. As we have seen, with the phenomenal growth of Tel Aviv in the 1920s and 1930s, Bialik's privacy was so curtailed that in 1933 he moved to the suburb of Ramat Gan to escape the constant stream of visitors.

From the turn of the century until his death he was an important figure in Hebrew publishing, and in the field of Jewish education was looked upon as a pre-eminent authority. His children's poems and stories include some of the loveliest in Hebrew, and over a hundred of his lyrics have been set to music. Bialik, in short, had charismatic appeal to everyone, from distinguished philosophers to small children learning Hebrew, and he spoke to all in their own language. Few poets have had such success as spokesman of a people, the representative of its cultural life and hopes. Why, then, did he feel such powerful self-reproach over his status as national poet? Why did he emphatically dismiss his public role?

Bialik's self-assessment as national figure is a central theme in his poetry. His protestations of his own unworthiness and inadequacy is, up to a point, familiar in Hebrew literature, especially the Biblical prophets, such as Amos, Isaiah and

Jeremiah. However, the guilt and self-denigration in Bialik are exceptionally sharp. He does not only reject his public role, he implies, and at times openly admits, that his chief motivations are private. As we have seen, too, most of his best poetry has nothing to do with the national cause. The sole poem in his *Collected Poems* from between 1916 and 1926, 'Shaḥa nafshi', was a reaction to the international celebration of his fiftieth birthday. Bialik echoes Amos (7: 14), but with a twist: 'I am no poet, no prophet / But a woodchopper'—i.e. a hired labourer doing a job, nothing more.

In fact, Bialik's insistence on the personal sources of his creativity and his ambivalence towards his role as 'prophet of revival' were already evident at the beginning of his career. In the only sonnet he is known to have written, in the early 1890s, he admitted that he was driven to write as a result of the poverty which he endured in childhood.[4] His cynicism at writing of Zion is put frankly in the poem 'Dimah Ne'emanah', written in 1894: 'When you see me weeping for some wondrous land...do not weep or comfort me, my tears are false.'[5] The motif of the poet tainted by a false prophecy returns in later poems, such as 'Davar' and *Megillat ha-Esh*.

Megillat ha-Esh appears to dramatize with particular force the conflicts which Bialik's national role stirred up in him. As we have seen, the poem begins with a cataclysmic account of the destruction of the second Temple in Jerusalem, but abandons national catastrophe to confess the ruin of one man, apparently the poet himself, by the fire of passion. The poem ends with a clear hint of the poet's guilt at being an imposter. What passes as the expression of national sorrow is, to a large extent, purely personal (*yegon ha-yaḥid*): an angel removes the poet's tears from the cup of national sorrow—they are tears of personal tragedy and do not belong in the national cup.

Bialik's art, like that of T. S. Eliot, was taken up by a movement which preferred to ignore—or remained ignorant of—the private, psychological reasons for writing, necessarily giving it instead a predominantly socio-political interpretation. And yet it is not always undesirable to be misread. Bialik was fascinated, as Eliot was, by the subtleties of revelation, concealment and

deception in language—knowing, as Eliot put it, that 'there may
be personal causes which make it impossible for a poet to express
himself in any but an obscure way.'[6] In the essay 'Giluy
ve-Khisuy be-Lashon', Bialik put forward the view that
'language in all its forms does not reveal its hidden meaning . . .
but serves as a partition, hiding it.'[7] The persona of national poet
was a convenient stay against over-inquisitiveness into his buried
life. In a late poem, 'Gam be-hitaroto le-eynekhem' (Even when
he wakes, 1931), he writes:

> Therefore he reveals himself, to be invisible and to deceive
> you. In vain you search the recesses of his verses—these too
> but cover his hidden thoughts . . .

While the excessive veneration led him to feel misunderstood,
and even perhaps restricted artistically, he might have been
thankful at times to hide beneath the protective mantle of
National Poet. A British psychiatrist, the late D. W. Winnicott,
found the same dilemma in all artists: 'The urgent need to
communicate and the still more urgent need not to be found.'[8]

Inevitably, Bialik's artistic instincts conflicted with his
national role. At the turn of the century, the growth of Hebrew
literature was unavoidably bound up with the rise of Jewish
nationalism. Though in a remarkably short time there would be
an eruption of Hebrew talent, in the 1890s really original
Hebrew poetry was scarce. In fact, not long beforehand, as the
Haskalah period was drawing to a close, Judah Leib Gordon, the
foremost Hebrew poet before Bialik, had lamented in his poem
'Le-Mi Ani Amel?' (For Whom Do I Labour?, 1871) that he
might be the last Hebrew poet. Bialik himself, as late as 1908, in
his essay 'Hevle Lashon' (Birthpangs of the Language), expressed
doubt as to whether Hebrew poetry would survive. By
becoming the first indisputably great Hebrew poet, Bialik
almost automatically became a cultural hero, with accompanying
responsibilities. The guilt which these responsibilities brought
upon him was exacerbated by his attachment to Ahad Ha'am, the
major influence upon his ideology. As we have seen, Ahad Ha'am
was convinced that Hebrew writers should forgo free creativity
and harness their energies to the national cause.

Bialik's friendship with the historian and critic Joseph Klausner, who helped launch him and later became professor of Hebrew Literature at the Hebrew University in Jerusalem, was undermined by his ambivalence towards his national role. 'As a poet,' Klausner wrote, 'Bialik did not take certain nationalist-Zionist obligations as seriously as I thought was right and proper for him.'9

Bialik had no ambitions to become a national institution, but this is exactly what happened in his lifetime. He shunned the idea of being celebrated by the people, feeling it to be undeserved. His first visit to Palestine, in 1909, started a wave of Bialik-mania; to his disgust he was mobbed by crowds of enthusiasts who saw him as their prophet of revival. Abraham Isaac Kook, who later became Chief Rabbi of Palestine, set the tone for his reception, greeting him rapturously in the name of the people: 'Sing from now, O poet beloved unto us, of the salvation of a people and its God, waken your harp. Be filled with the power and beauty to sing for us a song of the land, a song of rebirth.'10 To his wife, Bialik wrote from Jaffa, 'The people regard me as someone worthy of respect, but I know that I am a nothing, a nobody.'11

The fanfare which went on at the time of his fiftieth birthday weighed similarly on his conscience. At this time he published the opening chapter of *Safiah*, which ends with a dream of a solitary figure on a river bank and the poet's longing to break away from the crowd and become that figure once again. The dream on one level expresses the familiar tension between the poet's public and private identities. In the dream, the poet finds himself in a wilderness with a crowd of people returning from a fair:

I don't know how I come to be here or where I'm coming from. I walk on, swallowed up by one of the noisy crowds, dragged on almost without feeling. Tumult all round. Wagons and carts, laden or empty, drivers, leaders, passengers, men on horse and on foot, a throng of men and beasts, crawling wearily through sand and clouds of dust. Walking is hard as splitting the sea. Wheels and legs sink halfway in the sand. Dust. Heat. Everyone worn out, crushed, drenched in dirty sweat, miserable and angry— they're all yelling at their beasts, beating them cruelly. It seems that the fair had not gone well: no one got what he wanted. So they let it out on their poor beasts.[12]

Feeling that he is about to faint from the heat and tiredness, the poet is suddenly revived by a glimpse of a stream running behind a row of trees. He is certain that he alone can see it, and he longs to leave the crowd. But he keeps to the crowd in the wilderness, his eyes fixed on the trees. At this moment he has a miraculous vision, a tantalizing epiphany of a lost world, beyond his reach:

And now, the miracle! As I pass some of the more spindly, poorly spaced trees, I can look through and see a wonderful figure on the grass beside the stream. He sits alone, his back turned, contemplating the clear quiet water. The tumult of the crowd apparently does not reach him, it's as if he's in another world, far away. Motionless as a nail he sits, yet no matter how far I trudge on, he's there. I keep glimpsing his distant black figure between the trees, as if he and the pure stream and everything else were in motion with me, imperceptibly, like the moon in a river. Who is he? I do know him, don't I? We're so familiar, are we not? No matter what, I must get away to that pure peaceful world behind the green barrier. The bank of that clear stream is where I belong, isn't it? Hadn't I sat there, since long ago? —But I continue to drag along in the crowd, covered in dust, my ears ringing with noise. I move further and further away. Where are the trees by the river? Gone. Left behind with their pure world and clear stream and miraculous figure seated perpetually on the bank. Then I remember and my heart overflows with longing. That lonely figure whom I left on the riverbank— isn't he myself! My own self, no one else! --- [13]

This dream might be considered alongside 'Shaḥa nafshi', which addresses the poet's readers: 'My spirit is bowed to the dust / Under the yoke of your love'. He complains, with bitter humour, that he is used as a coin vulgarly jangling in the national coinbox. A startling metaphor, which appears in an unfinished poem,[14] of his poetry as illegitimate offspring, 'hybrid children of mixed seed... fruit of harlotry' might, among other things, reflect his guilt at writing personal poetry mistakenly thought to be national.

Bialik's apparent guilt at using national tragedy for personal aims might also, inadvertently, be reflected in *Be-Ir ha-Haregah*. For Bialik's chastisement of the cowardly, parasitical survivors, while it makes for extraordinary poetry—and shook the Jewish people in a way they needed at the time—does not do justice to the historical facts. Bialik was undoubtedly aware that the pogrom was as severe as it was precisely because some Jews did take up arms and defend themselves.[15] In the poem there is no mention of this. The opportunists who so infuriated Bialik were a minority, and their unheroic conduct did not warrant the emphasis which Bialik gives it. One explanation of this distortion is that Bialik, perhaps unconsciously, identified himself with the *schnorrers*, as he does elsewhere. In the poem 'Hirhure Laila', God chooses the poet to be a *schnorrer*-poet: 'Go round from door to door, knapsack on shoulder, go to the doors of generous men, bend down for a scrap of bread.'[16] Bialik's indignation with the *schnorrers* of Kishinev for using national tragedy for personal aims might have involved a displaced form of self-chastisement for doing something similar in his poetry. Out of the disaster in Kishinev he was making poetry—and advancing his career as 'National Poet'—as he had earlier out of the longing for Zion.

At the heart of Bialik's achievement lies the paradox that he was a national poet *par excellence* who suspected that he was bogus—and perhaps was so at times—and made poetry out of these suspicions. In this strange way, to paraphrase John Donne in his 'Third Satire', Bialik stood enquiring right, he doubted wisely. In the act of his self-doubt and self-undermining is the hard knowledge of his deepest ambiguities, the truth of his poetry.

6

POET OF PRIVATE GRIEF

Bialik's unease at being thought a national poet may be attributed partly to his awareness of personal factors in his creative life. Most important, it seems, the death of his father and the forced separation from his mother—far more than the rise of Jewish nationalism—were motivating forces and focal points of his later life as an artist, and although loss is only one of many factors in Bialik's art, the stress which he places upon his experience of bereavement is fully vindicated in recent studies of the effects of childhood loss, such as those of John Bowlby.[1] The emotional mainspring in a number of his poems in which the motif appears is identical with that of Wordsworth: both poets suffered the total break-up of their families at the age of seven. In the works of each, the death of a parent (in Wordsworth's case his mother) and the resulting separation from the surviving parent left lifelong scars and haunted the imagination.[2]

The effects of loss and family disruption are visible in many of the salient characteristics in the poetry of Bialik and Wordsworth: the intense preoccupation with childhood; the yearning for a lost paradise; the recurrent wish to become one with Nature; the general mood of isolation, desertion, depression, guilt and anger. The chief 'Romantic' quality of their poetry— the exploration of the self—may be seen as an attempt to buttress the self made weak by childhood loss and consequent emotional instability. Much of their greatest poetry tells of childhood: sections of Bialik's Safiaḥ, 'Ha-Brekha' and 'Eḥad eḥad' (One by one, 1915) are comparable with parts of Wordsworth's The Prelude, 'Tintern Abbey' and the 'Immortality' ode in their power to move.

Among the effects of childhood bereavement and separation was the heightening of the poets' response to the natural world, finding in it some of the attributes of parental love and care and the paradisal emblem of the lost time before the break-up of their families. Nature is often depicted in their works as a mother or nurse, a source of food from which they derive spiritual nourishment, consolation and peace. Both poets describe the first perception of the language and the bond of Nature in babyhood. In *Safiah* ch. 1, Bialik compares this language to the love which silently radiates from a mother to her child, constituting his bond with external reality:

> There was no speech and no words—only a vision. Such utterance as there was came without words or even sounds. It was a mystic utterance, especially created, from which all sound had evaporated, yet which still remained. Nor did I hear it with my ears, but it entered my soul through another medium. In the same way a mother's tenderness and loving gaze penetrate the soul of her baby, asleep in the cradle, when she stands over him anxious and excited—and he knows nothing.[3]

Wordsworth, too, connects the love of Nature with the love of the mother in babyhood:

> . . . blest the Babe
> Nursed in his Mother's arms, who sinks to sleep
> Rocked on his Mother's breast; who, with his soul
> Drinks in the feelings of his Mother's eye! . . .
> Along his infant veins are interfused
> The gravitation and filial bond
> Of Nature that connect him with the world.[4]

In trying to recreate and to understand their childhood, both poets may be expressing a wish to return to that time, to find comfort and stability in happy memories, and also, by confronting the trauma of loss, to engage in a form of self-analysis. Bialik's semi-mystical perception of the natural world may be linked with his loss;[5] and the need for a mystic bond with Nature is equally strong in Wordsworth. To Bialik, again, in 'Ha-Brekhah', this bond is expressed in a 'silent immanent language':

There is a secret language of gods, without sound, only shades of colour, made of magic, majestic pictures, hosts of visions. In this language God reveals himself to those he chooses, he meditates in it and uses it, creator that he is, to give body to his thoughts, to find the secret of the unformed dream. It is the language of images: a strip of blue sky and its expanse, the purity of small silver clouds and their dark mass, the tremor of golden wheat, the pride of the mighty cedar, the flap of the dove's white wing, the sweep of an eagle . . . the roar of a sea of flame, sunrise after sunset—in this language, tongue of tongues, the pool, too, formed me her eternal mystery.[6]

This language of natural beauty through which God communicates with his chosen ones is remarkably like that of the 'sense sublime' in Wordsworth's 'Tintern Abbey':

> And I have felt
> A presence that disturbs me with the joy
> Of elevated thoughts; a sense sublime
> Of something far more deeply interfused,
> Whose presence is the light of setting suns,
> And the round ocean and the living air,
> And the blue sky . . .

Both poets depict with unusual poignancy the loss of the childhood paradise and the failure of vision. Mid-life may have triggered off an artistic crisis:[7] shortly before reaching forty, both poets stopped writing poetry of childhood. In fact after 1808, when he was thirty-eight, Wordsworth's poetic inspiration deserted him; and after 1911, Bialik, at exactly the same age, practically stopped writing poetry, except for children. They mourn not only the 'visionary gleam' of childhood, but the premature loss of childhood itself:

> —But there's a tree, of many, one,
> A single field which I have looked upon,
> Both of them speak of something that is gone:
> The pansy at my feet
> Doth the same tale repeat;

Whither is fled the visionary gleam?
Where is it now, the glory and the dream?
Ode. Intimations of Immortality

My visions have fallen from me, my spirit is a stranger . . .
I know man drinks the golden cup but once,
And the vision will not come to him again.
For a sky so blue and grass so green,
The hidden light of the earth,
The shining face of God's works,
Grace the child's eye but once—never to return.
'Eḥad eḥad'

Another source of private grief in Bialik's poetry is his infertility, which, as has already been stated, is known to have troubled him deeply.[8] Bialik's preoccupation with the 'waste land' of his society is comparable with that of T. S. Eliot, in whom personal and social tragedy are fused similarly. The motif of infertility, particularly imagery of the waste land and the dead tree, appears relentlessly in Bialik's poems, most interestingly in lyrics such as 'Givole Eshtaked' and 'Tzanaḥ lo zalzal'.

The desert or desert island is depicted or alluded to in work after work, 'Mete Midbar', *Megillat ha-Esh*, 'Al kef yam-mavet zeh', *Safiaḥ* and *Aggadat Shlosha ve-Arba'ah*—to take only a few of the more prominent examples. As we saw earlier, 'Mete Midbar' alludes to the legendary warriors trapped in the desert after failing to enter the promised land:

The desert stretches
without life, without sound, without end.
The jubilant voice of the giants
is lost to the end of time.
The tumult of their footsteps
is gone forever.
Sandhills and crags remain where they trod.

The land in Eliot's poetry—*The Waste Land*, 'The Hollow Men', *Four Quartets*—is also consistently waste. 'Ash Wednesday' begins with a turn away from fertility—'I cannot drink / There,

where trees flower and springs flow'—and goes on to offer little
hope of change (in this life, at any rate), with its

> ... last desert between the last blue rocks
> The desert in the garden, the garden in the desert
> Of drought, spitting from the mouth the withered apple seed.

Imagery of the dead tree or branch, such as that in 'Tzanaḥ lo
zalzal', is found already in Bialik's juvenilia. In the poem 'Gesisat
Ḥole' (A Dying Man), written when Bialik was a teenager in
Zhitomir, he writes suggestively of a 'root of dust, a withered
flower ... a single nest of thorns and thistles, an empty shell, at
my loins the staff of an oppressor—is this the tree of life?'[9] The
dead tree is a familar sight in Eliot's poetry, too, occasionally
coupled with the dry stone:

> ... the dead tree gives no shelter
> And the dry stone no sound of water.
>
> *The Waste Land*

The works of Bialik and Eliot can be (and often are) taken to
reflect the barrenness of society, urgently in need of change. The
crisis of faith and the upheavals of their age—for Bialik, the
conditions in Russia following the pogroms of 1881–4 and of
1903–6; for Eliot, Europe devastated by the First World War—
could aptly be expressed in imagery of the waste land. However,
Bialik and Eliot adopted divergent attitudes toward their
respective traditions. For example, whereas to Bialik the violence
and injustices of the age undermined religious belief, to Eliot the
catastrophe of the First World War was an impetus to take
refuge in faith, Eastern as well as Western, and to shore the
fragments of tradition against ruin. Bialik did not place his faith
in any house of worship, but in the building of the Land of Israel.

The poetry of Bialik and Eliot may also be compared as
purely personal confessions. The infertility motif in their works
may be linked with the theme of childlessness which occurs in
their late works, in Eliot's *The Confidential Clerk* and in Bialik's
legends.[10] The desert landscape in their works might be
regarded, among other things, as the metaphoric landscape of
their childlessness. Whatever the reasons for their infertility,

there is no doubt that both, particularly Bialik, would have liked children. According to Bialik's wife Manya, the poet's love for children knew no bounds;[11] and Mrs Valerie Eliot, Eliot's second wife, has said that he was 'a naturally paternal man who should have had a large family'.[12] In both poets, the *kinnus*, or adoption, of fragments of culture may have taken the place of children; and their comparisons between creativity and childbearing have a particular poignancy.[13]

The infertility motif is one of many illustrations of the interconnection of the personal and the social or national in Bialik's writings. In this respect, too, Eliot's writings cast light on Bialik's art. Eliot was deeply aware that many writers—Dante, Shakespeare, Tennyson among them—in 'writing their time' were simultaneously making gigantic efforts to metamorphose private failures and disappointments. In his essay on Tennyson's *In Memoriam*, he wrote:

> It happens now and then that a poet by some accident expresses the mood of his generation, at the same time that he is expressing a mood of his own which is quite remote from that of his generation.[14]

In a similar vein, Bialik wrote of 'national' poetry in his essay 'Shiratenu he-Tze'ira' (Modern Hebrew Poetry, 1907):

> The private individual 'I' and the general national 'I' are swallowed up and blended one with the other, and you can't tell which came first and which is the more important.[15]

Bialik's art involves precisely such a synthesis of the private and the public. How was this synthesis reached?

7

CONCLUSION

The more we explore the personal sources of Bialik's creativity—especially in works such as 'Ha-Brekha', where he seems to turn his back on his national role—the more intimately we come to understand the underlying reasons for his impact as a national poet. His hypnotic appeal might be attributed precisely to the private obsessions which seem, on the surface, to have the least to do with Jewish nationalism.

The nature of Bialik's national role might, perhaps, be grasped more clearly by comparing him with another great national poet—Walt Whitman. The differences between Bialik and Whitman may well be more numerous and striking than the similarities, but in one vital respect their creativity has much in common: their national identity was bound up to a remarkable extent with purely personal trauma. Each poet in his own way evolved out of a unique fusion of the personal with the national. Whitman's fame rests almost entirely on one book of poems, *Leaves of Grass*, which was first published in 1855. In *Walt Whitman: The Making of the Poet*, the critic Paul Zweig has described in some detail the tortured conditions in which Whitman wrote. The poet, a middle-aged bachelor, was living at home in Brooklyn as his father lay dying in another room. Before that time he had shown little artistic talent: the flourishing of his genius seems to have been linked to a large extent with his father's death. It is estimated that a full two-thirds of Whitman's output was written in the year before and the year after this loss. His poetry served as a catharsis, a means of working through the grief process and of recreating himself. His new identity was that of America come-of-age, powerful, confident, creative, heir to the European tradition, to the 'corpse' that had fathered the New World. In the preface to *Leaves of*

Grass he wrote: 'America...perceives that the corpse is slowly borne from the eating and sleeping rooms of the house...that its action has descended to the stalwart and well-shaped heir who approaches'. Zweig notes the possible psychological link between the idea of America replacing Europe and Whitman taking his dying father's place and, in so doing, identifying himself with America: 'The son's self-willed rise had paralleled his father's decline, as if the empty place left by the father provided room for the son to change his life.'[1]

Bialik's national role involved an identification with the Jewish people not unlike that of Whitman with America. As an orphan, Bialik could best speak for his 'orphaned', uprooted people, express their sense of victimization and ruin, their sorrow, anger and frustration, and their longing to be reunited with their ancestral motherland. 'My might is that of the nation', he exclaims with Whitmanesque exuberance in the poem 'Iggeret Ketanah' (A Short Letter, 1894). He alludes to Ezekiel's vision of the dry bones resurrected:

> I too have power enough!
> In open spaces set free my imprisoned strength!
> A weak nation will blossom,
> My rotten bones will flourish like grass.

In depicting the national crisis of faith which troubled his age, Bialik used imagery of loss drawn from the recesses of childhood trauma, dimly remembered. The *deus absconditus* in poems such as 'Al ha-Shehitah', 'Davar' and *Megillat ha-Esh* is infused with rare power and pathos, which may be linked with the poet's loss of his father. The hope for the return of the wounded God in 'Yadati be-lel arafel' might have been connected in Bialik's mind with his hope for the return of his father. He never came to terms with his father's death. At the age of fifty he confessed in conversation that he thought of himself as 'an orphan who believes that a father does exist and that he might put in an appearance at any moment...this stems from weak nerves, from a certain ailment in the nervous system'[2]

Similarly, images of childhood loss and grief fill Bialik's poetry depicting Jewish symbols, customs and institutions. The

walls of the *bet midrash* in 'Al Saf Bet ha-Midrash' are compared
to 'silent mourners'. The holy fire preserved from the ruined
Temple in Jerusalem in *Megillat ha-Esh* is an 'orphaned lock'. The
once-holy books in 'Lifne Aron ha-Sefarim' are 'widowed'. Just
as the image of God is wounded, so also the image of the
Shekhinah is incapacitated. In 'Levadi' (Alone, 1902), the poet
finds himself alone in the *bet midrash* 'under the wings of the
Shekhinah':

> Alone, alone, I stayed,
>   the *Shekhinah* with me,
> dangling her right wing, broken
> upon my head. I knew:
>   she feared for me,
> her son, her only one.

> Driven from every corner,
>   she had just this last spot,
> tiny, desolate—the *bet midrash*—
> she hid in the shadows
>   and I
> joined her in grief.

While the *Shekhinah* in 'Levadi' is revered and worshipped, she is
also a harried, lonely, grieving presence, reminiscent of the
mother in 'Be-Yom stav', 'Shirati' (My Poetry, 1900–1) and
Yatmut. She, like the mother, cannot protect her son, but is herself
in dire need of help. And so, even in her presence, the poet is alone.

In the poetry, as we have seen, Bialik's separation from his
mother occupies a central place. This separation could not be
undone, but the wound of grief could be salved through striving
for national revival and the return to Zion. These aims
transcended private grief and took on independent significance.
Bialik's loss and separation from his mother gave the stamp of
intense conviction to his expression of national loss and the
yearning to return to Eretz Yisrael. In his speeches, Bialik
compared the yearning of the Jewish people to return to the
Land of Israel to the longing of a son to be reunited with his
mother after a long absence.[3] Already in his first published essay,

Bialik wrote of Zionism as a healing of spiritual sickness.[4]

The concept of cultural reunion, *kinnus*, seems also to have taken on particular force in Bialik's mind owing to his own experience of fragmentation in childhood. Having suffered complete family break-up by the age of eight, he preserved a lifelong need to put the pieces of his shattered life back together. He seems to have sublimated this need by attempting to bring together the fragments of the collective past of the Jewish people and make of them a new secular culture. In works such as 'Zohar', 'Eḥad eḥad' and *Safiaḥ* ch. 1, he uses Kabbalistic imagery of fading light or the lost sparks or flame to express the fall from childhood paradise. Identical imagery is found in his accounts of *kinnus*, the gathering of the lost sparks of national creativity, including his own, into a united national flame:

> From all the branches of our literature, from every corner in which a part of the 'holy spirit' of the nation is hidden, a part of the creativity of its best writers—we have to extract the best, scattered sparks, to join them together, to be united in the people's hand.[5]

In his conviction of personal artistic chosenness, too, Bialik inadvertently spoke to a people bound by a primordial sense of being chosen. The poem 'Ha-Brekha' may be read as a consummate expression of 'art for art's sake'. Creativity springs not from the hullabaloo of public life but in solitary stillness, such as that of the figure by the riverbank in *Safiaḥ* ch. 1. In the language of Nature, through which God communicates with his 'chosen ones', the pool speaks to the poet of the eternal mystery of creation:

> Seeing all, all seen in her, she changes
> with everything. She seemed to me like the open eye
> of the forest-lord rich in mystery
> and long long thoughts.

The sense of being chosen, on a personal level as in the national sphere, may be understood as one means of compensating for grievous loss.

The parallels between personal and national grief in Bialik's life and works may be pursued further. The 'Poems of Wrath', as already indicated, may express the rage felt by the orphaned child as well as that of an 'orphaned' people. The low self-esteem expressed by the orphaned poet in works such as 'Ve-Haya ki timtze'u' and 'Vi-Yhi mi ha-ish' may be seen as the personal equivalent of the sense of inferiority suffered by a people bereft of its homeland. Bialik's intense idealization of the lost woman, the mother or mother-figure, runs parallel with the idealization of Zion in his works (which draws heavily on the portraits of Zion in the Bible and *aggadah*). Even his poetry of despair provides insight into his power as a national poet: only someone who had looked despair in the face could offer hope to a people whose future must at times have seemed hopeless. The tears of the poet, we see strikingly in *Megillat ha-Esh*, are so commingled of personal and national causes that, as Bialik put it, 'you can't tell which came first and which is the more important'.[6] Even as a poet of grief and doom, rather than of hope and revival, Bialik spoke with the voice of his people, challenging them to prove him wrong.

Finally, as national poet Bialik could project on to his people his feelings of impotence, infertility and inferiority as well as strive in a symbolic form for the fertility denied to him personally. Thus the poet could write of the Jewish people using imagery similar to that with which he described himself in poems such as 'Tzanaḥ lo zalzal'. In 'Akhen ḥatzir ha'am' he characteristically berates his people:

> Will dew revive a dead leaf off a tree,
> or hyssop clinging to rocks, or a broken vine,
> a dry flower? Can trumpet blasts and a raised banner
> revive the dead?

Elsewhere, however, especially in his essays and speeches, he depicts the national revival with imagery of flowering and fruitfulness.

The extent of the correlation between the personal and the national in Bialik's art is astonishing. On the most basic level, Bialik's national appeal involved a mutual appeal for help, and a simple collective and individual response to this cry.

CONCLUSION

More clearly than most poets, Bialik bears out Lionel Trilling's contention that 'the elements of art are not limited to the world of art... anything we may learn about the artist himself may be enriching and legitimate.'[7] Bialik is the principal subject of his poetry, a Romantic tormented by what he had lost in life (or never had) and could never regain. With astonished reluctance, he adopted the voice of a people whose perpetual mourning for its lost nationhood was enhanced and given fresh meaning by a profound social and religious crisis. The elegiac tone of his poetry is that of the Jewish people in exile. The wrath in his poetry marks the beginning of a great transition which would lead fourteen years after Bialik's death to the creation of the Jewish state. Bialik's private agonies and hopes mirrored national trauma and revival in such an extraordinary way that the two became intertwined and inextricably linked in the poetry.

NOTES

Unless otherwise indicated, all translations are my own. Biblical quotations are from the Revised Standard Version.

Introduction

1 Richard Ellmann, *Yeats: The Man and the Masks*, Faber, London, 1969, p. 2. The conflict in Bialik between the 'man of reverie' and the public 'man of action' is depicted most strikingly in the allegorical dream in *Safiah* ch. 1. See ch. 5 below.
2 In the first of three unsent drafts of an autobiographical letter from Bialik to Joseph Klausner, written in mid-1903. *Ketavim Genuzim shel C. N. Bialik* (Posthumous Works), p. 232. The final draft of this letter is included in *Iggrot C. N. Bialik* (Letters) 1: 157–73.

1: *The Man and the Legend*

1 Recounted by J. Fichman, *Shirat Bialik* (Bialik's Poetry), pp. 380–1.
2 The main sources for biographical information on Bialik are F. Lachower, *Bialik: Hayyav vi-Tzirotav* (Life and Works) and *Iggrot C. N. Bialik* (Letters). Further sources are given in the Bibliography pp. 134–5.
3 For a portrait of Bialik's grandfather, see *Ketavim Genuzim shel C. N. Bialik* (Posthumous Works), pp. 225–7.
4 'Avi' is the first in the four-part cycle, *Yatmut* (Orphanhood). On *Yatmut*, see below, ch. 4.
5 'By nature I am similar both to my father and to my mother. My father was quiet and spiritual, though he suffered a lot. My mother was full of bitterness and noise. These two lines of personality are prominent in me.' Quoted by C. Glicksberg, *Bialik Yom Yom* (Bialik in Daily Life), p. 85.
6 *Iggrot* 1: 3.
7 *Ketavim Genuzim*, p. 240. Bialik's mischievousness as a child might have been connected with his experience of loss, as an expression of protest and of the need for consistent and benevolent parental authority: 'If I climbed to the top of a telegraph pole—blows! If I

went sliding across the ice—more blows! If I crowed like a rooster on the roof at midnight—blue murder!' *Iggrot* 1: 158. The poet Zalman Schneour once noticed that Bialik had lost a number of teeth. He asked him how it happened. Bialik replied that they had been knocked out when he was showing off to his friends as a child and he leaped from the roof of his grandfather's house. J. Fichman, ed., *Sefer Bialik* (The Bialik Book), p. 19. Manya Bialik, the poet's wife, was fond of telling of an incident which occurred when Bialik was about nine or ten. 'He climbed a tree and shouted "Fire! Fire!" Naturally everyone came running and when it turned out to be a false alarm they wanted to punish him. He sat perched on this tall tree and no one could reach him. Afterwards, he climbed down and hid behind one of the houses for an entire day without food or water.' *Pirke Zikhronot* (Memoirs), p. 11. She also told how he used to maltreat his sister, Hannah Judith, who had joined him at his grandfather's house several months after his arrival: '... there were frequent arguments. Sometimes she would get angry and he would take revenge by tossing out all her things from the closet.' *Ibid.* As he was a difficult child, he was vulnerable to the onslaughts of relatives who had a notion of how to 'civilize' the boy: 'In times of "emergency", when my weak old grandfather couldn't manage me, uncles and cousins would come by, out of pity for the orphan, to beat him in the name of heaven and teach him manners.' *Ketavim Genuzim*, p. 240. One of these relatives is described in Bialik's letter to Klausner: 'I had an uncle, young and stupid, and when I misbehaved he would take me to the toilet and whip me, laughing as he did so. I was so ashamed that I hid my anger and told no one.' *Iggrot* 1: 159.

8 *Ketavim Genuzim*, pp. 225–6.
9 *Ibid.*, p. 242.
10 This article, entitled 'Al Ra'ayon ha-Yishuv' (On the Idea of Settlement [in the Land of Israel]), was published in *Ha-Melitz* on 9 Nisan (17 April NS) 1891, and is reprinted in *Ketavim Genuzim*, pp. 229–31.
11 *Ibid.*, p. 241.
12 *Iggrot* 1: 168–9.
13 *Ibid.*, pp. 137–8. This letter finds an echo in the poem 'Davar'. See ch. 4.
14 *Kol Kitve Chaim Nachman Bialik* (Collected Works), 1-vol. edn., p. 192. The nihilism of 'Giluy ve-Khisuy be-Lashon' has its poetic counterpart in 'Hetzitz va-Met' (He Looked and Died), written during the same period. An English translation of 'Giluy ve-Khisuy be-Lashon' appears in R. Alter, ed., *Modern Hebrew Literature*, pp. 130–7.

[15] 'The Reluctant Laureate', *The Sunday Times*, 14 October 1984, p. 39.

[16] *Iggrot* 1: 274.

[17] Manya Bialik, *Pirke Zikhronot* (Memoirs), p. 29.

[18] *Iggrot* 2: 189–90.

[19] *Pirke Zikhronot*, p. 25.

[20] *Iggrot* 2: 240.

[21] *Ibid.* 3: 95.

[22] *Ibid.*, pp. 105, 107.

[23] *Pirke Zikhronot*, p. 43.

[24] *Iggrot* 5: 310.

[25] In H. Orlan, ed., *Shirat C. N. Bialik: Anthologia* (Bialik's Poetry: an Anthology), p. 370.

[26] Ben-Gurion, too, was deeply influenced by Bialik. In his memoirs, he recalled that Bialik was 'the poet, the beloved of my soul'. As a young man, he would copy Bialik's poems, as they appeared in the journals, into a notebook and learn them by heart. *Bet Avi* (Father's House), Hakibbutz Hameuchad, Tel Aviv, 1974, pp. 34–5.

[27] Cf. M. Ungerfeld, *Bialik ve-Sofre Doro* (Bialik and the Writers of his Generation), p. 124.

[28] In V. Mayakovsky, *The Bedbug and Selected Poetry*, M. Hayward, G. Reavey, trs., Weidenfeld & Nicolson, London, 1961, p. 129.

[29] *Pirke Zikhronot*, p. 22.

[30] The fullest bibliography on Bialik to date is that of M. Ungerfeld, *C. N. Bialik vi-Tzirotav* (Bialik and his Works). An outline of bibliograpical sources is given by Y. Arnon in H. Barzel and M. Michelson, eds., *Me'asef·10: Yetzirot Chaim Nachman Bialik* (Essays on Bialik), pp. 98–110.

2: *The Background*

[1] On the history and conditions of the Jews in Tsarist Russia, see S. Dubnow, *History of the Jews*, 5 vols., M. Spiegel tr., Thomas Yoseloff, New York, 1967–1973 (orig. 1925–9); L. Greenberg, *The Jews in Russia: The Struggle for Emancipation*, Yale University Press, New Haven & London, 1965 (orig. 1944) and S. Baron, *The Russian Jew Under Tsars and Soviet*, Macmillan, London & New York, 1976. For a clear general history of Russia under the Romanovs, see R. Pipes, *Russia under the Old Regime*, Weidenfeld & Nicolson, London, 1974.

[2] Quoted by D. W. Treadgold, *The West in Russia and China*, Cambridge University Press, 1973, vol. 1, p. 181.

[3] *Kol Kitve Chaim Nachman Bialik* (Collected Works), p. 225. For a poetic expression of these sentiments, see 'Im-yesh et-nafshekha la-da'at' (If you want to know, 1897).

4 *Ketavim Genuzim shel C. N. Bialik* (Posthumous Works), p. 236.
5 Tr. I. M. Lask, *Aftergrowth and other stories*, p. 89.
6 See ch. 1 above and *Ketavim Genuzim* pp. 225–6.
7 *Ibid.*, p. 241.
8 On Hasidism and the Kabbalah, see G. Scholem, *Major Trends in Jewish Mysticism*, Schocken Books, New York, 1974 (orig. 1941). For further discussion of Bialik's use of Kabbalah imagery, see below.
9 On the literary and historical background to Bialik's writings, see J. Klausner, *Historia shel ha-Sifrut ha-Ivrit ha-Hadasha* (History of Modern Hebrew Literature), 6 vols., Ahiasaf, Jerusalem, 1952–8; and S. Halkin, *Modern Hebrew Literature: Trends and Values*, Schocken Books, New York, 1950. Further background material is given in the Bibliography.
10 A comprehensive study of European Romanticism is to be found in H. G. Schenk, *The Mind of the European Romantics*, Constable, London, 1966.
11 J. Talmon, *Romanticism and Revolt—Europe 1815–1848*, Thames & Hudson, London, 1967, p. 96.
12 A full account of the pogroms is given by Dubnow, op. cit.
13 For a history of the Zionist movement, see D. Vital, *The Origins of Zionism* and *Zionism: The Formative Years*, Clarendon Press, Oxford, 1975, 1982.
14 'Rabi Zarah' is included in the standard textual edition of Bialik's poems, *C. N. Bialik: Shirim* (Poems: 1890–8), ed. D. Miron *et al.*, pp. 320–2.
15 Bialik's degree of Jewish observance varied at different times in his life, but it seems that he generally did observe the Sabbath and the dietary laws. In 1926, he said: 'I am not an orthodox Jew in the accepted sense of the word, but I am happy with religious education.' *Devarim she-Be'al Peh* 1: 85. However, the scholar Shimon Rawidowicz, who knew Bialik in the 1920s, wrote that he 'profaned the Sabbath in private and in public'. *Sihot im Bialik*, p. 95.

3: *Literary Roots*

1 *Iggrot C. N. Bialik* (Letters) 2: 109.
2 On Bialik's use of Hebrew sources, see Tzippora Kagan, in H. Barzel and M. Michelson, eds., *Me'asef·10: Yetzirat Chaim Nachman Bialik* (Essays on Bialik), pp. 84–92.
3 *Devarim she-Be'al Peh* (Speeches) 1: 45.
4 Cf. F. Lachower, *Bialik: Hayyav vi-Tzirotav* (Life and Works), pp. 734–5.
5 On Bialik's sources in *Va-Yhi ha-Yom*, see M. ben-Ezekiel, in G.

Shaked, ed., *Bialik: Yetzirato le-Sugeha bi-Re'i ha-Bikoret* (Essays on Bialik), pp. 337–72.

6 These legends are recounted by Bialik and Ravnitzky, eds., *Sefer ha-Aggadah* (The Book of Legends), 1-vol. edn., 1973, pp. 47, 55–6. For further discussion of 'Akhen gam zeh musar Elohim' and its rabbinical sources, see F. Lachower, op. cit., p. 499. Lachower also includes a most interesting account of Ahad Ha'am's influence on this poem. *Ibid.* pp. 500–3.

7 A more plausible version of this well-known anecdote is given by A. B. Rhine in *Leon Gordon*, Jewish Publication Society, Philadelphia, 1910, pp. 155–6n.

8 *Kol Kitve Chaim Nachman Bialik* (Collected Works), 1-vol. edn., p. 231.

9 On European and Russian influences on Bialik, see Lachower, op. cit.

10 Introduction to Turgenev's *Fathers and Sons*, tr. R. Edmonds, Penguin Classics, Harmondsworth, 1978, p. 12.

11 'Art for its own sake, giving pleasure for its own sake, has its place and value in life; but in our present state, we believe that our meagre literature should not waste its strength on such things at a time when there are other, more pressing and useful matters at hand.' Ahad Ha'am, 'Te'udat *Ha-Shiloah*.' (The Aim of *Ha-Shiloah*), *Ha-Shiloah* (1896) 1: 5.

12 Tr. D. Patterson, from *Safiah* ch. 1, *The Jewish Quarterly* (1973) 20, 4: 17. See ch. 6, note 5 below.

13 *Ha-Sipporet ha-Ivrit: 1880–1970* (Hebrew Fiction. 1880–1970), p. 99.

14 *Shirat Bialik* (Bialik's Poetry), p. 383.

15 See, for example, *Kol Kitve Mendele Mokher Sefarim* (Collected Works), p. 176.

16 *Devarim she-Be'al Peh* 2: 191. This volume contains six of Bialik's speeches on Ahad Ha'am. On Ahad Ha'am's influence on Bialik, see Aliza Klausner Baer, in Barzel and Michelson, eds., op. cit., pp. 315–33.

17 On Bialik's 'fatal encounter' with Ahad Ha'am, see Dov Sadan, in Shaked, ed., op. cit., p. 19.

18 *Devarim she-Be'al Peh* 2: 209. On the *Shekhinah*, see ch. 4, note 26 below.

4: *Romantic-National Poet*

1 On Bialik's use of metre, see Benzion Benshalom, in G. Shaked, ed., *Bialik: Yetzirato le-Sugeha bi-Re'i ha-Bikoret* (Essays on Bialik), pp. 52–81. It is interesting that, according to Benshalom, only three of Bialik's poems were written in the Sephardic pronunciation; the rest

are in the Ashkenazic pronunciation which, among other things, tends to stress the syllable before the last whereas in the Sephardic pronunciation the last is stressed more often.

2   In this connection, it is relevant to mention that Bialik chose to open his collection of Yiddish poems (1913) with the poem 'Glust sich mir weinen' (When I want to cry), in which he identifies his mother's tears as a possible source of his creativity.

3   On Odessa, see Steven J. Zipperstein, *The Jews of Odessa: a cultural history 1794–1881*, Stanford University Press, 1985.

4   Nevertheless, in 1901 Bialik published a Yiddish poem, 'Dos Letzte Wort', (The Last Word), which anticipates the 'Poems of Wrath', particularly 'Davar'. On this poem, see F. Lachower, *Bialik: Hayyav vi-Tzirotav* (Life and Works), pp. 391–7.

5   Interestingly, though, both 'Al ha-Shehitah' and *Be-Ir ha-Haregah* attack God. The first expresses the poet's doubt whether there is a God (apparently for the first time in Hebrew poetry), for he would not allow such atrocities as the Kishinev pogrom, or at least he would punish the evildoers. In the second, Bialik taunts the pogrom victims with the famous lines which were originally cut by the Russian censor as they were considered too blasphemous: 'Your God is as poor as you, / Poor as you in life, how much more in death.' Yet in the later poem 'Yadati be-lel arafel' the poet holds out the hope that the God of Vengeance will reveal himself at the end of time, and justice will prevail. (On the *deus absconditus* in Bialik as a possible reflection of Bialik's loss of his father and the hope of his return, see the Conclusion below.) Bialik's attacks on God have precedents in Jewish literature. For example, in the Talmud, anger is expressed at the supposedly omnipotent God over the destruction of the Temple in Jerusalem by Titus:

> Abba Hanan says: '"Who is mighty as thou art, O Lord" [Psalms 89: 8]. Who is powerful and hard as you, for you hear the abuse and blasphemy of that wicked man [Titus] and you remain silent.' In the name of Rabbi Ishmael it was taught: 'Who is like you, O Lord, among the gods [elim]' [Exodus 15: 11]. Who is like you among the silent [ilmim].' (*Gittin* 56b)

6   Tr. A. M. Klein, in I. Efros, ed., *Poetic Works of H. N. Bialik*, p. 127.

7   In Bialik's *Collected Poems*, 'Akhen gam zeh musar Elohim' is erroneously dated Tammuz (i.e. summer) 1905. See Lachower, op. cit., p. 493.

8   See the poems 'Be-Yom stav', 'Shirati' and *Yatmut*, and the autobiographical prose account in *Ketavim Genuzim shel C. N. Bialik*

(Posthumous Works), pp. 237–8.

9 *Iggrot C. N. Bialik* (Letters) 2: 1.

10 Note to *A Choice of Shakespeare's Verse*, Faber, London, 1971, p. 181.

11 In the depiction of sexual matters, Bialik was a puritan. In a letter to Joseph Klausner (*Iggrot* 1: 186–7), he wrote that he loathed the expression of youthful sexual feelings by Hebrew writers. Apart from 'Ha-Eynayim ha-re'evot', forceful descriptions of sexual disgust in Bialik are found in *Megillat ha-Esh*, 'Haya Erev ha-Kayitz' (On a Summer's Evening, 1908), and *Ketavim Genuzim* pp. 164, 168, 184–5.

12 This poem appears in the 'Tosefet' (Supplement) to *Kol Kitve Chaim Nachman Bialik* (Collected Works), pp. 368–9. For the poem with textual variants, see *Chaim Nachman Bialik: Shirim* (Poems: 1890–8), ed. D. Miron *et al.*, pp. 221–3.

13 N. Goren, *Pirke Bialik* (On Bialik), p. 35.

14 See D. Aberbach, 'Childlessness and the Waste Land in C. N. Bialik and T. S. Eliot', *Hebrew Union College Annual* (1984), 55: 283–307.

15 *Iggrot* 1: 172.

16 Cf. John Bowlby, *Loss: Sadness and Depression* (vol. 3 of *Attachment and Loss*), The Hogarth Press and the Institute of Psycho-Analysis, London, 1980, for a full account, with bibliography, of the possible effects of childhood loss such as that suffered by Bialik.

17 See, for example, *Mikhtavim el Ra'ayato Manya* (Letters to Manya his Wife), p. 126.

18 M. Ovadiahu, *Mi-Pi Bialik* (Conversations with Bialik), p. 35.

19 See ch. 3 above.

20 B. Kurzweil has suggested that the madonna-prostitute syndrome underlies this episode of *Megillat ha-Esh*, that the girl at the top of the cliff represents the madonna and her reflection is the whore: *Bialik ve-Tchernichovsky* (Bialik and Tchernichowsky), p. 48 ff. On the possible links between this phenomenon and the motif of orphanhood in Bialik, see D. Aberbach, 'Screen Memories of Writers', *International Review of Psycho-Analysis* (1983), 10, 1: 48–50.

21 The imagery of the tear-filled cup appears to be based on Psalms 56: 9: see ch. 3 above. Similar imagery is found in the poems 'Hirhure Laila' and 'Birkhat Am'.

22 *Devarim she-Be'al Peh* (Speeches) 2: 26.

23 Quoted by M. Ungerfeld, *Bialik ve-Sofre Doro* (Bialik and the Writers of his Generation), p. 141.

24 *Devarim she-Be'al Peh* 2: 30.

25 On similar memories of Bialik and other writers, see D. Aberbach, 'Screen Memories of Writers', op. cit.

26 The *Shekhinah*, according to Jewish legend, is the feminine presence

of God wandering with the Jews through the Diaspora. Cf. G. Scholem, *Major Trends in Jewish Mysticism*, Schocken Books, New York, 1974, pp. 229–33.

27 A fascinating account of this visit in Yiddish (with Hebrew translation) appears in *Mikhtavim el Ra'ayato Manya*.

28 See John Bowlby, op. cit.

29 J. H. Ravnitzky, 'Reshimot Pinkas al C. N. Bialik' (Notebook Jottings on Bialik), *Reshumot* (1946), 2: 182. Bialik's wish for death in childhood was associated with the stove in his grandfather's house: 'Here, by this warm fire ... if my eyes were to close forever, if I were to sleep an eternal sleep—could there be greater pleasure?' (*Iggrot* 1: 162)

30 *Iggrot* 2: 46. Yet, as Amos Elon has written, 'None before Bialik nor after has expressed the Jewish will to live in words and rhymes of such beauty and poetic force...' *The Israelis: Founders and Sons*, Bantam Books, New York, 1972, p. 162.

31 *Iggrot* 2: 174.

32 Cf. E. Jacques, 'Death and the Mid-Life Crisis', *International Journal of Psycho-Analysis* (1965) 46: 502–14.

33 *Iggrot* 2: 103.

34 *Ibid.*, p. 119.

35 *Pirke Bialik*, op. cit., p. 32.

36 C. Glicksberg, *Bialik Yom Yom* (Bialik in Daily Life), p. 85.

37 Tr. I. M. Lask, *Aftergrowth and other stories*, pp. 71, 72. It is noteworthy that this section of *Safiah* (ch. 2–7), in which the little boy is constantly seeking and finding objects to suck and chew on, was written during the same period as the darkest poems of despair.

38 Tr. Lask, op. cit., p. 97. Rashi (Rabbi Solomon ben Yitzhak, 1040–1105) has been the most popular Jewish exegete from the Middle Ages until the present day: see ch. 2 above. The biblical passage referred to is Genesis 28: 11. Among other works which depict the effect of *aggadah* on Jewish children in eastern Europe, see Mendele Mokher Sefarim, *Ba-Yamim ha-Hem* (In Those Days); M. J. Berdichewsky, 'Ha-Yetziah' (The Departure); and S. J. Agnon, 'Ha-Mitpahat' (The Kerchief).

39 *Iggrot* 2: 249.

40 Tr. D. Patterson, from *Safiah* ch. 1, *The Jewish Quarterly* (1973) 20, 4: 17.

41 *Ibid.*

42 *Kol Kitve Chaim Nachman Bialik*, p. 352.

43 Though 'Avi' is highly sympathetic to the father, Bialik's depiction of the father or father-figure, whether real or imagined, is almost always fraught with tension and fear. See, for example, *Safiah*, ch. 2

and 5 as well as the posthumous chapter and *Ketavim Genuzim*, p. 174 ff. In 'Me-Aḥore ha-Gader', the father beats his recalcitrant son so badly that he spends two months recuperating in bed.
44 See Bowlby, op. cit.

5: National Figure

1 Chaim Weizmann, *Trial and Error*, p. 544.
2 Chaim Chernowitz, *Masekhet Zikhronot* (Book of Memories), p. 129. For Rashi, see ch. 4, note 38 above.
3 *Kol Kitve Chaim Nachman Bialik* (Collected Works), p. 227. A translation of this speech appears in A. Hertzberg, ed., *The Zionist Idea: A Historical Analysis and Reader*, Harper and Row, New York, 1959, pp. 281–8.
4 'Ha-Shirah me-Ayin ti-Matzeh' (Whence will the Poetry Be Found, 1893), a parody of Gordon, opens with the line, 'My Lord made me a poet-merchant', and ends, 'No Jew sings [i.e. writes poetry] except from poverty.' *Chaim Nachman Bialik: Shirim* (Poems: 1890–8), ed. D. Miron *et al.*, p. 229.
5 Bialik's uncertainty over the wisdom of making such a confession may be evident in the poem's omission in the 1908 collection of his poetry.
6 T. S. Eliot, *The Use of Poetry and the Use of Criticism*, Faber, London, 1975, p. 150.
7 *Kol Kitve Chaim Nachman Bialik*, p. 191.
8 D. W. Winnicott, *The Maturational Processes and the Facilitating Environment*, The Hogarth Press and the Institute of Psycho-Analysis, London, 1975, p. 185. It appears that the first to put forward the view that literature is a disguised form of self-expression was the Victorian clergyman and poet John Keble: indeed, according to M. H. Abrams, this is his chief historical importance. Keble writes that the impulse to express one's emotions is 'repressed by an instinctive delicacy which recoils from exposing them openly as feeling that they never can meet with full sympathy.' This creates a conflict in poets between the need for release from inner pressure and reticence and shame at self-exposure, a conflict which threatens them with insanity. Poetry is a divinely inspired medicine, able to satisfy opposed motives by giving 'healing relief to secret mental emotion, yet without detriment to modest reserve.' It is, therefore, 'the art which under certain veils and disguises...reveals the fervent emotions of the mind.' Quoted by Abrams, *The Mirror and the Lamp*, p. 147. All this is relevant in understanding Bialik's poetry and his view, expressed in 'Giluy ve-Khisuy be-Lashon', that the purpose of language is to conceal. In conversation, similarly, Bialik spoke of the

psychology of the artist driven to seek emotional release in his art, yet tormented by having revealed himself:

> Mostly, he feels terrible regret, immediately or afterwards, that he has revealed to a stranger his personal secrets... And then he gets very angry not only at himself for having exposed his weakness, but also at the one who saw him exposed... Together with this, he hates the man for having brought about this misfortune... He's ashamed so he runs away from the one who saw him—he doesn't want, isn't able, to face him.
>
> (M. ben Eliezer, 'Mi-Siḥotav shel Bialik' [Conversations with Bialik], *Knesset* (1941) 6: 92.)

Among the poems which touch on this difficulty and connected ones, see 'Ve-Haya ki timtze'u' and 'Vi-Yhi mi ha-ish'.

9   *Knesset* (1937) 2: 114.
10 Quoted by M. Ungerfeld, *Bialik ve-Sofre Doro* (Bialik and the Writers of his Generation), p. 259.
11 *Mikhtavim el Ra'ayato Manya* (Letters to Manya his Wife), p. 40.
12 *Kol Kitve Chaim Nachman Bialik*, p. 147. In his allegorical use of the image of the fair, Bialik was almost certainly thinking of Shalom Aleichem's autobiography, *Fun Yarid* (From the Fair).
13 *Ibid.*, pp. 147–8. In conversation, Bialik would connect the figure on the riverbank with his own childhood. F. Lachower, 'Ḥayyav' (Bialik's Life), *Moznayim* (1934), 2: 398.
14 *Ketavim Genuzim shel C. N. Bialik* (Posthumous Works), p. 148.
15 Cf. I. Heilpern, in H. Orlan, ed., *Shirat C. N. Bialik: Anthologia* (Bialik's Poetry: An Anthology), p. 221.
16 See D. Aberbach, 'On Re-reading Bialik: Paradoxes of a "National Poet"', *Encounter* (June 1981) 56, 6: 42.

6: *Poet of Private Grief*

1   See ch. 4, note 16 above.
2   Cf. D. Aberbach, 'Loss and Separation in Bialik and Wordsworth', *Prooftexts* (May 1982) 2, 2: 197–208. On loss in Wordsworth, see R. J. Onorato, *The Character of the Poet: Wordsworth in the Prelude*, Princeton University Press, 1971; A. Brink, 'On the Psychological Sources of Creative Motivation', *Queen's Quarterly: A Canadian Review* (Spring 1974) 81, 1: 1–19; and J. Wordsworth, *William Wordsworth: The Borders of Vision*, Clarendon Press, Oxford, 1982.
3   Tr. D. Patterson, *The Jewish Quarterly* (1973) 20, 4: 17.
4   *The Prelude* II, 234–7, 242–4; 1850 edn.
5   See D. Aberbach, 'Grief and Mysticism', *International Review of*

Psycho-Analysis (1987) 14, 4.
The almost mystical importance which Bialik attached to childhood memories may be compared with that of Wordsworth. 'Here before me on this backcloth of blue skies and green grass', he writes in *Safiaḥ* ch. 1,

> are embroidered the pictures of my world, those first days, wonderful pictures, light and calm as pure mists, half secrets and half dreams—and nevertheless no scenes as bright and clear as they are, nor any reality as real. They are my soul's basic elemental scenes, bestowed upon me freely from the skies, a gift of God and His goodness, because of my tender years and helplessness, my dumbness and my heart's pining. (Tr. D. Patterson, op. cit. See ch. 3 above.)

Yet other early memories, which Bialik did not include in any of his written accounts of his childhood, reveal a totally different side of the child's life: 'Children are cruel by and large. I recall one of the gentiles in our village, a drunkard. He'd roll with the pigs in the mire. We despised him. We would gang up on him and fill his mouth with horse manure and similar things.' (C. Glicksberg, *Bialik Yom Yom* [Bialik in Daily Life], p. 113.) In another conversation, Bialik recalled the sanitary conditions in Radi and the pigs:

> I've had an instinctive hatred of pigs since childhood. Like all Jewish children, I was disgusted by them. In our village only the rich had private toilets. The children would go behind the fences, any place where they couldn't be seen. The pigs would come and stick their snouts into the urine and excrement. I would torment them by staring at them and by throwing pebbles at their filthy snouts. (*Ibid.*, p. 57).

6 In 'Ha-Brekha', the pool is 'the symbol of the creative spirit'. Letter from Bialik to Ira Jahn, quoted by M. Ungerfeld, *Bialik ve-Sofre Doro* (Bialik and the Writers of his Generation), p. 139.

7 See ch. 4, note 32 above.

8 Cf. D. Aberbach, 'Childlessness and the Waste Land in C. N. Bialik and T. S. Eliot', *Hebrew Union College Annual* (1984) 55: 283–307.

9 *Chaim Nachman Bialik: Shirim* (Poems: 1890–8), ed. D. Miron *et al.*, p. 234.

10 See D. Aberbach, 'Childlessness and the Waste Land in C. N. Bialik and T. S. Eliot', op. cit., pp. 284–6.

11 See Glicksberg, *Bialik Yom Yom*, p. 24.

12 Personal communication to David Aberbach, Mrs T. S. Eliot.

13 See, for example, *Devarim she-Be'al Peh* (Speeches) 2: 25; and T. S. Eliot, *On Poetry and Poets*, Faber, London, 1975, p. 99.

14 In F. Kermode, ed., *Selected Prose of T. S. Eliot*, Faber, London 1975, p. 243.

15 *Kol Kitve Chaim Nachman Bialik* (Collected Works), p. 234. See Conclusion below.

Conclusion

1 P. Zweig, *Walt Whitman: The Making of the Poet*, Viking Penguin, New York, 1984, p. 237.

2 H. Greenberg, 'A Day with Bialik', in M. Syrkin, ed., *Hayyim Greenberg Anthology*, p. 307.

3 *Devarim she-Be'al Peh* (Speeches) 1: 159. See also ch. 5 above.

4 *Ketavim Genuzim* (Posthumous Works), p. 229.

5 *Kol Kitve Chaim Nachman Bialik* (Collected Works), p. 196.

6 *Ibid.*, p. 234. See ch. 6 above.

7 L. Trilling, *The Liberal Imagination*, Penguin, Harmondsworth, 1970, p. 61.

BIBLIOGRAPHY

The Bet Bialik in Tel Aviv has the largest collection of Bialikana in the world, but these holdings have not yet been published. The fullest bibliography to date is M. Ungerfeld's *C. N. Bialik vi-Tzirotav* (Bialik and His Works), Dvir, Tel Aviv, 1960. This work contains information on most of Bialik's works as well as the main critical writings on Bialik until 1960. An outline of bibliographical sources is given by Y. Arnon, 'Mekorot la-Bibliographia shel Chaim Nachman Bialik' (Bibliographical Sources on Bialik), in Barzel and Michelson, eds., *Me'asef·10: Yetzirat Chaim Nachman Bialik* (Essays on Bialik), Massada, Tel Aviv, 1975, pp. 98–110.

Works by Bialik

Kitve C. N. Bialik u-Mivhar Targumav (The Works of C. N. Bialik and Selected Translations [including Cervantes' *Don Quixote* and Schiller's *Wilhelm Tell*]), 4 vols., Hotza'at Hoveve ha-Shirah ha-Ivrit, Berlin, 1923.

Kol Kitve Chaim Nachman Bialik (Collected Works), 19th edn, Dvir, Tel Aviv, 1958. Does not include the translations, children's poems, speeches, letters, Yiddish poems or posthumous writings.

Chaim Nachman Bialik: Shirim (Poems: 1890–8), ed. D. Miron *et al.*, Dvir & Katz Research Institute for Hebrew Literature, Tel Aviv, 1983. The standard critical edition. Vol. 2 in preparation.

Shirim u-Fizmonot li-Ladim (Poems and Songs for Children), 4th edn, Dvir, Tel Aviv, 1971 (orig. 1933).

Shirav ha-Idiyim (Yiddish Poems), tr. A. Zeitlin, Dvir, Tel Aviv, 1956 (orig. Yiddish publication 1913).

Ketavim Genuzim shel C. N. Bialik (Posthumous Works), ed. M. Ungerfeld, Dvir, Tel Aviv, 1971.

Devarim she-Be'al Peh (Speeches), 2 vols., Dvir, Tel Aviv, 1935.

Iggrot C. N. Bialik (Letters), ed. F. Lachower, 5 vols., Dvir, Tel Aviv, 1937–9.

C. N. Bialik: Iggrot el Ra'ayato Manya (Letters to Manya his Wife), Mossad Bialik and Dvir, Tel Aviv, 1955.

BIBLIOGRAPHY

'Iggrot el Ahad Ha'am' (Letters to Ahad Ha'am), *Knesset* (1942)
7: 15–27.
*Halifat Iggrot ben S. Y. Abramowitz u-Ven C. N. Bialik u-Ven Y. H.
Ravnitzky* (Correspondence between Abramowitz, Bialik and
Ravnitzky), ed. C. Shmeruk, Israeli National Academy of Sciences,
Jerusalem, 1974.
Bialik, C. N., tr., *Ben Shne Olamot* (Ansky's *The Dybbuk*), *Ha-Tekufah*
(1918) 1: 222–96.
Bialik, C. N., tr., Shakespeare's *Julius Caesar*, Act I, scenes 1–3,
Moznayim (1929) 1, 3: 2–5; 1, 7: 6–9.
Bialik, C. N. & Ravnitzky, J. H., eds., *Sefer ha-Aggadah: mivhar
ha-aggadah sheba-Talmud uva-Midrash* (The Book of Legends: a
selection from the Talmud and Midrash), 5th edn, Dvir, Tel Aviv,
1973 (orig. 1908–10).
Bialik, C. N. & Ravnitzky, J. H., eds., *Shire Shlomo ben Yehuda ibn
Gabirol* (The Poems of Solomon ibn Gabirol), 3 vols. in 7 parts,
Dvir, Tel Aviv, 1927, 1929, 1932.
Bialik, C. N. & Ravnitzky, J. H., eds., *Shire Moshe ben Ya'akov ibn Ezra*
(The Poems of Moses ibn Ezra), 2 vols., Dvir, Tel Aviv, 1928. The
poems of ibn Gabirol and ibn Ezra are the subject of letters which
Bialik sent to J. Marcus, in Marcus' *Iggrot Bialik be-Noge'a le-Hotza'at
Shire Rabbi Shlomo ibn Gabirol ve-Rabbi Moshe ibn Ezra*, Jewish
Publication Society, Philadelphia, 1935.
Bialik, C. N., ed., *Seder Zera'im shel Shisha Sidre Mishna* (Order *Zera'im*
['Seeds'] of the Six Orders of the Mishna), Dvir, Tel Aviv, 1957
(orig. 1932).

English Translations

Danby, H., tr., *And It Came to Pass* [*Va-Yhi ha-Yom*], Hebrew
Publishing Company, New York, 1938.
Danby, H., tr., *Knight of Onions and Knight of Garlic* [*Aluf Batzlut ve-Aluf
Shum*], Jordan Publishing Company, New York, 1939.
Efros, I., ed., *Poetic Works of H. N. Bialik*, Bloch Publishing Company,
New York, rev. edn., 1965 (orig. 1948).
Lask, I. M., tr., *Aftergrowth and other stories*, Jewish Publishing
Company, Philadelphia, 1939. D. Patterson has done a translation
from *Aftergrowth* ch. 1, *The Jewish Quarterly* (Winter 1973) 20,
4: 17–18.
Nevo, R., tr., *Chaim Nachman Bialik: Selected Poems* [bilingual], Dvir &
The Jerusalem Post, Jerusalem, 1981.
Snowman, L. V., ed., *Chaim Nachman Bialik: Poems from the Hebrew*,
Hasefer, London, 1924.

BIALIK

For further bibliography of individual works in English translation, see Y. Goell, *Bibliography of Modern Hebrew Literature in English Translation*, Jerusalem, Israel University Press, 1968. Updated annually by the Institute for the Translation of Hebrew Literature, Tel Aviv, ed. I. Goldberg.

Anthologies Containing Selections of Bialik's Poetry

Burnshaw, S., Carmi, T., & Spicehandler, E., eds., *The Modern Hebrew Poem Itself* [bilingual], Schocken Books, New York, 1966.
Carmi, T., ed. & tr., *The Penguin Book of Hebrew Verse* [bilingual], Penguin Books and Allen Lane, New York & Harmondsworth, 1981.
Finer-Mintz, R., tr., *Modern Hebrew Poetry: a bilingual anthology*, University of California Press, Berkeley & Los Angeles, 1968.

Biographical Works

Bialik, M., *Pirke Zikhronot* (Memoirs), Dvir, Tel Aviv, 1963.
Chernowitz, C., ('Rav Tzair'), *Masekhet Zikhronot* (Book of Memories), Shulsinger, New York, 1945.
Fichman, J., *Shirat Bialik* (Bialik's Poetry), Mossad Bialik, Jerusalem, 1946.
Glicksberg, C., *Bialik Yom Yom* (Bialik in Daily Life), Hakibbutz Hameuchad, Tel Aviv, 1945.
Glusman, S., *Ben ha-Mozeg: Sippur Hayyav shel ha-Meshorer Chaim Nachman Bialik* (Son of the Taverner: The Life of the Poet Bialik), Joseph Sreberk, Tel Aviv, 1970.
Goren, N., *Pirke Bialik* (On Bialik), N. Twersky, Tel Aviv, 1949.
Greenberg, H., 'A Day with Bialik', in *Hayyim Greenberg Anthology*, ed. M. Syrkin, Wayne State University Press, Detroit, 1968.
Klar, B., *Bialik: Leben für ein Volk*, Josef Belf, Vienna, 1936.
Klausner, J., 'Ha-Hartza'ah ha-Pumbit ha-Rishonah al Bialik ve-Toza'oteha' (The First Public Lecture on Bialik and Its Consequences), *Knesset* (1937) 2: 113–20.
Klausner, J., 'Chaim Nachman Bialik', *Encyclopedia Hebraica* 8: 239–57.
Kleinman, M., 'Im Bialik le-Moskva' (To Moscow with Bialik), *Davar*, 25.9.1936; 2.10.1936; 9.10.1936; 16.10.1936; 23.10.1936; 30.10.1936; 6.11.1936; 4.12.1936.
Kressel, G., 'Chaim Nachman Bialik', in *Lexicon ha-Sifrut ha-Ivrit ba-Dorot ha-Aharonim* (Lexicon of Modern Hebrew Literature), vol. 1, Sifriat Poalim, Tel Aviv, 1965, pp. 199–219.
Lachower, F., 'Hayyav' (Bialik's Life), *Moznayim* (1934) 2: 394–419.

134

Lachower, F., *Bialik: Hayyav vi-Tzirotav* (Life and Works), 3 vols., Mossad Bialik & Dvir, Tel Aviv, 4th edn, 1964 (orig. 1944–8). The standard edition. Reaches 1908.

Leiter, S., & Spicehandler, E., 'Hayyim Nachman Bialik', *Encyclopedia Judaica* 4: 795–803.

Ovadiahu, M., *Mi-Pi Bialik* (Conversations with Bialik), Aleph, Tel Aviv, 1969.

Ravnitzky, J. H., *Dor ve-Sofrav* (Writers I Have Known), 2 vols., Dvir, Tel Aviv, 1926, 1937.

Ravnitzky, J. H., 'Reshimot Pinkas al C. N. Bialik', (Notebook Jottings on Bialik), *Reshumot* (1946) 2: 182–7.

Rawidowicz, S., *Sihotai im Bialik* (Conversations with Bialik), ed. Y. Friedlander & B. C. I. Ravid, Dvir, Tel Aviv, 1983.

Schneour, Z., *C. N. Bialik u-Vne Doro* (Bialik and His Contemporaries), Am Oved, Tel Aviv, 1953.

Ungerfeld, M., *Bialik ve-Sofre Doro* (Bialik and the Writers of his Generation), Am Hasefer, Tel Aviv, 1974.

Hebrew Criticism

Individual Works

Aberbach, D., 'Bialik ve-Wordsworth: Shirat ha-Yaldut' (Bialik and Wordsworth: Poetry of Childhood), *Moznayim* (July 1977) 45: 102–12.

Adar, Z., *Bialik be-Shirato* (Bialik in his Poetry), Newman, Jerusalem, Tel Aviv, 1967.

Avineiri, Y., *Milon Hiddushe C. N. Bialik* (A Dictionary of Bialik's Innovations in Hebrew), Zvi Casp, Tel Aviv, 1935.

Avital, A., *Shirat Bialik veha-Tenach* (Biblical Allusions in Bialik's Poetry), Dvir, Tel Aviv, 1952.

Bakon, Y., *Ha-Prozodia shel Shirat Bialik* (Bialik's Prosody), Ben-Gurion University, Beersheba, 1983.

Becker, J., 'C. N. Bialik vi-Tzirotav le-Or ha-Psychoanaliza' (A Psychoanalytic View of Bialik), pamphlet, Deah, Sifriya Psycho-analytit, Jerusalem, 1931.

Even-Shoshan, A. & Segal, Y., *Concordantzia le-Shirat Bialik* (Concordance to Bialik's Poems), Kiryat Sefer, Jerusalem, 1960.

Ezekiel, M. ben, 'Sefer *Va-Yhi ha-Yom*' (On *And It Came to Pass*), *Knesset* (1941) 6: 29–63.

Fichman, J., *Shirat Bialik* (Bialik's Poetry), Mossad Bialik, Jerusalem, 1946.

Klausner, J., *Bialik ve-Shirat Hayyav* (Bialik and his Poetry), Dvir, Tel Aviv, 1950.

Kurzweil, B., *Bialik ve-Tchernichovsky* (Bialik and Tchernichowsky), Schocken, Tel Aviv, 1975.

Mazya, A., *Bialik ha-Eḥad: Be-Sovkhe Parshanut u-Meḥkhar* (Bialik the One: In the Thicket of Interpretation and Research), Reshafim, Tel Aviv, 1978.

Miron, D., *Ha-Predah min ha-Ani he-Ani: mahalakh be-hitpatḥut shirato ha-mukdemet shel Chaim Nachman Bialik 1891–1901* (Departure from the Impoverished 'I': the development of Bialik's early poems of 1891–1901), Everyman's University, Tel Aviv, 1986.

Peri, M., *Ha-Mivne ha-Semanti shel Shire Bialik* (Semantic Structure in Bialik's Poetry), Tel Aviv University, 1977.

Sadan, D., 'Al ha-Ner ha-Daluk' (The Burning Candle), *Knesset* (1938) 3: 79–87.

Sadan, D., 'Ben Ma'ayan le-Yuvlav' (Essays on Bialik), in *Avne Gader* (Essays), Massada, Tel Aviv, 1970.

Schweid, E., *Ha-Ergah le-Malot ha-Havayah* (The Yearning to Fill Existence), Massada, Tel Aviv, 1968.

Shamir, Z., *Ha-Tzeratzar Meshorer ha-Galut: al ha-yesod ha-amami bi-tzirat Bialik* (Poet of Exile: on the national origins of Bialik's poetry), Tel Aviv University, 1986.

Shapira, Z., *Derakhim be-Shirat Bialik* (Interpretations of Bialik), Emesh, Tel Aviv, 1965.

Shapira, Z., *C. N. Bialik: bi-Netivot Shirato* (Interpretations of Bialik), Emesh, Tel Aviv, 1974.

Tsur, R., *Devarim ka-Havayatam: Iyunim be-Shirat Bialik* (Studies of Bialik's Poetry), Sifre Dagah, Tel Aviv, 1963.

Zemah, A., *Ha-Lavi ha-Mistater: Iyunim bi-Tzirato shel Chaim Nachman Bialik* (The Lion in Hiding: Studies on Bialik), Kiryat Sefer, Jerusalem, 1966.

Anthologies

Barzel, H., & Michelson, M., eds., *Me'asef·10: Yetzirat Chaim Nachman Bialik* (Essays on Bialik), Massada, Tel Aviv, 1975.

Fichman, J., ed., *Sefer Bialik* (The Bialik Book), Jubilee Committee & Amanut, Tel Aviv, 1934.

Lachower, F., et al., eds., *Knesset*, 11 vols., 1936–46, 1969, Mossad Bialik, Jerusalem.

Orlan, H., ed., *Shirat C. N. Bialik, Anthologia: Mivḥar divre pesher, ha'arakha, massot, divre-levai, ve-zikharon al kol shire Bialik* (The Poetry of Bialik: an anthology of commentaries and interpretations of each poem and selected essays and studies on the poet), Dvir, Tel Aviv, 1971.

Shaked, G., ed., *Bialik: yetzirato le-sugeha bi-re'i ha-bikoret* (Essays on Bialik), Mossad Bialik, Jerusalem, 1974.

English Criticism

Aberbach, D., *A Study of the Writings of C. N. Bialik with some comparative aspects*, M. Litt. thesis, Oxford University, 1977.

Aberbach, D., 'Screen Memories of Freud, Bialik, and Wordsworth', *Midstream* (October 1979) 25, 8: 39–43.

Aberbach, D., 'On Re-reading Bialik: Paradoxes of a "National Poet"', *Encounter* (June 1981) 56, 6: 41–8.

Aberbach, D., 'Loss and Separation in Bialik and Wordsworth', *Prooftexts* (May 1982) 2, 2: 197–208.

Aberbach, D., 'Poet of the People', *Jewish Chronicle* 29.6.1984, p. 28.

Aberbach, D., 'Childlessness and the Waste Land in C. N. Bialik and T. S. Eliot', *Hebrew Union College Annual* (1984) 55: 283–307.

Alter, R., 'The Kidnapping of Bialik and Tchernichovsky', in *After the Tradition*, E. P. Dutton & Co., New York, 1969.

Bateson, M. C., '"A Riddle of Two Worlds": An Interpretation of the Poetry of H. N. Bialik', *Daedalus* (1966) 95: 740–62.

Patterson, D., 'Chaim Nachman Bialik', in *The Foundations of Modern Hebrew Literature*, The Liberal Jewish Synagogue, London, 1961.

Yudkin, L., 'The Quintessence of Bialik's Poetry and its Significance', in *Escape into Siege*, Routledge & Kegan Paul and the Littman Library of Jewish Civilization, London, 1974.

Literary and Historical Background

Alter, R., ed., *Modern Hebrew Literature*, Behrman House, New York, 1975.

Halkin, S., *Modern Hebrew Literature: Trends and Values*, Schocken Books, New York, 1950.

Klausner, J., *Historia shel ha-Sifrut ha-Ivrit ha-Hadasha* (History of Modern Hebrew Literature), 6 vols., Ahiasaf, Tel Aviv, 1952–8.

Mendes-Flohr, P. R., & Reinharz, J., eds., *The Jew in the Modern World: A Documentary History*, Oxford University Press, New York & Oxford, 1980.

Patterson, D., *The Hebrew Novel in Czarist Russia*, Edinburgh University Press, 1964.

Pipes, R., *Russia under the Old Regime*, Weidenfeld & Nicolson, London, 1974.

Zborowski, M., & Herzog, E., *Life is With People: The Culture of the Shtetl*, Schocken Books, New York, 1974 (orig. 1952).

INDEX OF BIALIK'S WORKS

Italics designate longer works; an asterisk indicates that the work is translated in its entirety; dates and titles in English are given at first reference.

Aggadat Shelosha va-Arba'ah, 92, 111
'Aḥare moti', 14,* 37
'Akhen gam zeh musar Elohim', 45, 65–7,* 124, 125
'Akhen ḥatzir Ha-am', 39–40, 41–2
'Al ha-Sheḥitah', 42, 61–2,* 66, 115, 125
'Al-kef yam-mavet zeh', 54, 82, 111
'Al levavkhem she-shamem', 79
'Almenut', 94–5; see *Yatmut*
'Al Ra'ayon ha-Yishuv', 3, 121
'Al Saf Bet ha-Midrash', 57, 116
Aluf Batzlut ve-Aluf Shum, 47, 101, 133
'Arvit', 82*
'Aryeh Ba'al Guf', 7, 52
'Avi', 2, 13, 94, 120, 127; see *Yatmut*
'Avim Ḥoshrim', 93
'Ayekh?', 73, 82

'Bar Kochba', 50; see 'En zot, ki rabat tzerartunu'
'Be-Ginat ha-Yarak', 93
Be-Ir ha-Haregah, 7, 15, 33, 34–5, 42, 50, 62, 63, 98, 107, 125
Ben Shne Olamot (tr. *The Dybbuk*), 101, 133
'Be-Yom stav', 57, 74, 82, 116, 125
'Birkhat Am', 56, 97, 126

'Davar', 42, 63–5*, 66, 67, 73, 103, 115, 121, 125
'Dos Letzte Wort', 125
'Dimah Ne'emanah', 57, 103
Don Quixote (tr.), 101, 132
The Dybbuk (tr.); see *Ben Shne Olamot*

'Eḥad eḥad', 108, 111, 117
'El ha-Aryeh ha-Met', 48
'El ha-Tzippor', 4, 46, 57
'En zot, ki rabat tzerartunu', 17, 50
'Eyneha', 57

Folk Poems; see *Shire Am*

'Gam be-hitaroto le-eynekhem', 104
'Gesisat Ḥole', 112
'Giluy ve-Khisuy be-Lashon', 6, 104, 121, 128
'Givole Eshtaked', 72–3,* 111
'Glust sich mir weinen', 125

'Ha-Brekha', 8, 108, 109–10, 114, 117, 130
'Ha-Eynayim ha-Re'evot', 69–70,* 126
'Ha-Ḥatzotzra Nitbaysha', 10, 32
'Ha-Kayitz gove'a', 40–1
'Hakhnisini taḥat kenafekh', 74
'Halaila aravti', 40,* 71
'Halakhah ve-Aggadah', 10
Ha-Matmid, 5, 23–4
'Ha-Sefer ha-Ivri', 9
'Ha-Shirah me-Ayin ti-Matzeh', 103, 128
'Haya Erev ha-Kayitz', 126
'Hem mitna'arim me'afar', 79–81*
'Hetzitz va-Met', 46, 57, 121
'Ḥevle Lashon', 104
'Hirhure Laila', 39, 107, 126
'Holekhet at me-imi', 74, 78, 82
'Ḥoze lekh beraḥ', 42–3

'Iggeret Ketanah', 115
'Im dimdume ha-ḥamah', 71–2*
'Im-yesh et-nafshekha la-da'at', 122

'La-Mitnadvim ba-Am', 56, 57, 97–8
'Le-Aḥad Ha'am', 54
'Levadi', 116
'Lifne Aron ha-Sefarim', 57, 81, 116
'Li-Netivekh ha-ne'elam', 78, 82
'Lo herani Elohim', 83
'Lo zakhiti ba-or min ha-hefker', 58

'Manginah le-Ahavah', 70
'Masah Nemirov', 50; see *Be-Ir ha-Haregah*
'Me-Aḥore ha-Gader', 9, 52, 127
'Me-Aḥore ha-Sha'ar', 93
Megillat ha-Esh, 8, 9, 13, 25, 43–4, 63, 74, 75–9, 82, 100, 103, 111, 115, 116, 118, 126
'Mete Midbar', 44, 97, 111
'Mete Midbar ha-Aḥaronim', 97
'Mi ani u-mah ani', 83–4*
'Mikhtav katan li katva', 70–1
'Mi-Shire ha-Ḥoref', 51
'Mi-Shut ba-Merḥakim', 57
'Mi yode'a ir Lishtina?', 59

'Poems of Wrath'; see *Shire Za'am*
'Predah', 13, 74, 95–6; see *Yatmut*

'Rabi Zaraḥ', 34, 123
'Raze Laila', 57–8

Safiaḥ, 9, 10, 22–3, 50, 52, 53, 89–92, 105–6, 108, 109, 111, 117, 127
'Sefer Bereshit', 92–3
Sefer ha-Aggadah (co-editor), 8–9, 31, 43, 101, 123
'Shaḥa nafshi', 46, 103, 106
'Shiratenu ha-Tze'ira', 113
'Shirati', 116, 125
'Shirat Yisrael', 57
Shire Am (Folk Poems), 9, 31, 38, 48, 59, 101
Shire Za'am ('Poems of Wrath'), 8, 16, 33, 45, 60–9, 75, 76, 99, 100, 118, 125
Shirim u-Fizmonot li-Ladim, 12, 92
'Shiva', 94; see *Yatmut*
'Tzanaḥ lo zalzal', 87,* 89, 92, 111, 118

Va-Yhi ha-Yom, 12, 43, 92, 123, 133
'Ve-Haya ki timtze'u', 45 6, 84–5,* 93, 118, 129
'Ve-Haya ki ya'arkhu ha-yamim', 42

'Ve-Im yishal ha-malakh', 73–4
'Vi-Yhi mi ha-ish', 85–6,*, 88,
  118, 129

Wilhelm Tell (tr.), 11, 101, 132

'Yadati be-lel arafel', 41, 68–9,*
  79, 115, 125

'Yam ha-demamah polet sodot',
  36, 59–60*
Yatmut ('Avi', 'Shiva', 'Almenut', 'Predah'), 13, 82, 87, 89,
  94–6, 116, 120, 125; see under
  individual entries

'Zohar', 91, 117

GENERAL INDEX

Abramowitz, S. J., see Mendele Mokher Sefarim

Agnon, Samuel Joseph, 15, 52, 127

Ahad Ha'am, 3, 8, 12, 25, 34, 50, 53–5, 59, 82, 98, 99, 100, 101, 104, 124, 132

Alexander II, Tsar, 27, 32

aliya, 1st, 5, 33–4; 2nd, 34; 3rd, 35

Ansky, S., 101, 133

anti-Semitism, 19, 20–1, 27, 28, 31–3, 38, 45, 53, 60 ff., 98, 99

Ba'al Shem Tov (Israel ben Eliezer), 24

Babel, Isaac, 59

Balfour Declaration, 11, 35

Belinsky, Vissarion, 21, 50

Ben-Ami, M. (Rabinowitz), 67

Ben Zion, S., 59, 88

Berdichewsky, M. J., 8, 48, 127

Berlin, 5, 11, 90

bet midrash, 22, 23, 99, 116

Bialik, Dinah Priva (mother), 1, 2, 13, 58, 88–9, 94–6, 108, 120

Bialik, Hannah Judith (sister), 121

Bialik, Jacob Moses (paternal grandfather), 1, 2–3, 23, 77, 81, 82, 95–6, 120, 121

Bialik, Joseph Isaac (father), 1, 2, 13, 53, 63, 66, 94, 95, 108, 115, 120

Bialik, Manya (wife, *née* Aver-bach), 4–5, 9, 10, 11, 16, 70, 71, 75, 105, 113, 121

Bible, 3, 5, 6, 22, 29, 30, 35, 37, 39–43, 70, 76–7, 91, 99, 102–3, 115, 118, 127; see *Chumash*

Black Hundreds, 32, 67

Brenner, Joseph Chaim, 15

Bund, 35

censorship, 43, 49–50

Chaadaev, Peter, 21

Chaim of Volozhin, 24–5

Chernowitz, Chaim (Rav Tzair), 98

Chernyshevsky, Nikolai, 21

Chumash (Pentateuch = Five Books of Moses), 3, 22, 26, 41; see Bible

Crimean War, 27, 32

Dostoevsky, Fyodor, 15, 20

Dreyfus, Alfred, 34

Dubnow, Simon, 59, 83

Dvir, 11, 12; see Moriah

Eliot, T. S., 39, 56, 58, 103, 104, 111–3

Enlightenment, 26, 29; see *Haskalah*

Ezra, Moses ibn, 12, 46, 101

Feierberg, M. Z., 48

Feodosiya, 67

Fichman, Jacob, 52, 59, 88
Frug, Simon, 48

Gabirol, Solomon ibn, 12, 46, 101
Gnessin, Uri Nissan, 15
Goethe, Johann Wolfgang von, 48
Gogol, Nikolai, 16, 20, 48, 52
Gomel, 34
Gordon, Judah Leib, 38, 47–8, 104, 124
Goren, Nathan, 88
Gorky, Maxim, 11, 16
Gorovshchin, 7, 62
Greenberg, Uri Zvi, 16

Halevi, Judah, 46, 99
Ha-Me'asef, 26
Ha-Shahar, 31
Ha-Shiloah, 7, 8, 15, 34, 50, 54, 55, 67
Hasidism, 19, 24–5, 26, 99, 123
Haskalah (Enlightenment), 19, 24, 26–9, 38, 39, 46, 47–8, 99, 104
Hebrew University, 12, 100
heder, 22–3, 28, 90, 99
Heine, Heinrich, 48
Herder, Gottfried, 30–1
Herzl, Theodor, 5, 15, 34, 63
Hibbat Zion, 4, 33, 34, 54

Jabotinsky, Ze'ev (Vladimir), 7, 15, 16
Jahn, Ira (Slyapin), 78, 130
Jerusalem, 11, 24, 50, 75, 77, 100, 103, 116
Jews, assimilation of, 28, 45, 65–6; self-defence of, 34–5, 68
Judaism, 53, 63, 79, 81, 100–1, 125

Kabbalah, 24, 25, 38, 102, 117, 123
Khmelnitsky, Bogdan, 20, 50
Kiev, 5, 7
kinnus, 9, 101–2, 113
Kishinev, 7, 34, 60, 61–2, 74, 125
Klausner, Joseph, 8, 18, 54, 74, 105, 120, 121
Kook, Abraham Isaac, 105
Korosten, 5, 59

Lachower, Fischel, 18
Lamdan, Isaac, 14
Lermontov, Mikhail, 48
Lessing, Gotthold Ephraim, 48
Levin, Shmaryahu, 12
Lilienblum, M. L., 4, 47

Maimonides (Moses ben Maimon), 37
Mapu, Abraham, 47
Mayakovsky, Vladimir, 16
May Laws, 32, 33
Melitopol, 67
Mendele Mokher Sefarim (S. J. Abramowitz), 15, 51–3, 59, 99, 101, 127
Mendelssohn, Moses, 26
Mitnagdim, 24
Moriah, 7, 9; see Dvir
Moscow, 10
Moznayim, 12

Nicholas I, Tsar, 21, 31, 32, 33, 47
Nicholas II, Tsar, 63
Nietzsche, Friedrich, 48

Odessa, 4, 7, 8, 11, 32, 33, 48, 52, 54, 56, 58–9, 60, 67–8, 78, 79, 82, 88, 98, 125
Oneg Shabbat, 12

Pale of Settlement, 19 ff., 27, ˹3,

32, 33, 34, 59, 99, 122
Peretz, Isaac Leib, 75
Pinsker, Leon, 33
pogroms, 7, 8, 10, 11, 28, 31–3, 34, 35, 51, 60 ff., 98, 112, 123
Poland, 19, 20, 30
Polish revolt, 20, 28, 32
Potemkin mutiny, 8, 63, 78
Protocols of the Elders of Zion, 31, 67
Pushkin, Alexander, 20, 29, 48

Radi (Radomyshl), 1, 2, 50, 89, 130
Ramat Gan, 13, 102
Rashi, 22, 90, 98, 101, 127
Ravnitzky, J. H., 4, 5, 8, 12, 46, 59, 82, 88, 123
Romanovs, 20, 122
Romanticism, 19, 29–30, 48, 56 ff., 108 ff., 123
Russian Civil War, 33
Russian revolution, 10, 16–17, 19, 35, 49, 52
Russo-Japanese war, 33, 63, 67

Sadan, Dov, 18, 54
Schiller, Friedrich, 29, 48, 97, 101
Schlegel, Friedrich, 29
Schneour, Zalman, 15, 59, 120–1
Scholem, Gershom, 38, 102
serfs, freeing of, 32
Shabbetai Zvi, 24
Shalom Aleichem, 129
Shalom, Shin, 15
Shekhinah, 54, 81, 116, 126
Shimoni (Shimonowitz), David, 15
Shlonsky, Abraham, 15
Shoffman, Gershon, 15
shtika, 9, 56, 57, 87–9, 110

Smolenskin, Peretz, 31, 47
Sosnowiec, 7, 59

Talmud and Midrash, 8–9, 12–13, 22, 23, 31, 36, 37, 38, 43–6, 49–50, 53, 73, 76, 90, 92, 99, 118, 125, 127
Tchernichowsky, Saul, 15, 48
Tel Aviv, 11, 13, 38, 102
Tolstoy, Leo, 20, 48
Turgenev, Ivan, 20, 49

Ungerfeld, Moshe, 15, 132

Vienna, 10, 13, 31
Vilna Gaon (Eliezer ben Solomon Zalman), 24
Volhynia, 1, 8, 19, 24, 50
Volozhin, 3, 4, 5, 23, 24, 48, 53, 77, 99

Warsaw, 7, 8, 67, 73
Weizmann, Chaim, 12, 15, 98
Whitman, Walt, 114–5
Wissenschaft des Judentums, 99
Wordsworth, William, 1, 29, 87, 91, 97, 108–11, 129

Yeats, W. B., xii, 58
Yiddish, 7, 21, 26, 38, 51, 99, 124–5, 132
Yitzhak, Avraham ben, 11

Zashkov, 2
Zhitomir, 1, 2, 4, 23, 67, 78, 95, 99, 112
Zionism, 3, 4, 5, 11, 12, 15, 17, 19, 25, 28–9, 30–1, 33–5, 48, 49, 53–4, 56, 59, 63, 79, 81, 97 ff., 112, 116–7, 121, 123
Zunz, Leopold, 47